THE SILENT PARTNERS

Daniel Jay Baum
and Ned B. Stiles

The Silent Partners

INSTITUTIONAL
INVESTORS AND
CORPORATE CONTROL

SYRACUSE UNIVERSITY PRESS

To Harriet and Janet

PREFACE

For ease of reading an effort was made to avoid excessive citation. For the statistical data included herein with respect to the size, growth, portfolio make-up, and market activities of institutional investors, the authors are principally indebted to the following sources, in addition to those noted throughout this work: The New York Stock Exchange, Institutional Shareownership: A Report on Financial Institutions and the Stock Market (1964); The Wharton School of Finance and Commerce, A Study of Mutual Funds, Prepared for the Securities and Exchange Commission (1962); Securities and Exchange Commission Statistical Series Releases: No. 1902, Corporate Pension Funds, 1962 (May 24, 1963), No. 1978, Private Non-Insured Pension Funds, 1963 (June 4, 1964), No. 1986, Volume and Composition of Individuals' Savings, January-March, 1964 (June 30, 1964).

This work had its beginnings in 1960 when one of the authors submitted a manuscript titled, "Institutional Investors: A Check on The Management of the Giant Corporation," in partial fulfillment of the degree of Doctor of Juridical Science at New York University's School of Law. Since then the seeds of an idea grew, blossomed, and ripened into this substantially different endeavor. Nevertheless, for his patience and guidance in connection with the dissertation, deep appreciation is extended to Dean Miguel A. de Capriles of New York University. Our thanks also to Paul P. Harbrecht, S.J., Dean of the School of Law, University of Detroit, for his Introduction, to our wives for their consideration and encouragement, and, finally, to Mrs. Vonda Lutz who typed and retyped so many drafts.

Indiana University DANIEL JAY BAUM
New York City NED B. STILES
Winter 1965

INTRODUCTION

The problem of economic power that results from the large size of modern enterprise, the structure of industry, the influence of our financial institutions are all matters of public policy, going to the question of what kind of society we want to live in. As things now stand there is no clear goal or national criterion which we can use to determine whether modern changes are leading us where we want to go. Federal and state courts and legislatures and innumerable agencies and departments deal with the problem every day, and the conclusions they reach depend very much on the philosophy of each individual charged with the responsibility of making, interpreting, or administering the laws that govern the conduct of business. One conclusion that can be drawn from the evidence presented in *The Silent Partners* is that not to choose a course of conduct along which industry shall be directed, but to leave the vital questions of bigness, industry structure, and size and impact of financial institutions to the natural functions of the evolutionary process, is to make a very grave choice indeed. Not to act or establish a norm is to allow a structure to arise with which we will have to live whether we like it or not. An economic system cannot simply be dismantled by the stroke of a pen in some law we may one day decide to enact.

Careful reading of the work of Professor Baum and Mr. Stiles provides us with a good object lesson in the process of natural accretion by which a society shapes itself. Business and industry begin to take a certain course; that course is curbed and regulated but not stopped or reversed. Governmental agencies are established for the protection and assertion of the public interest and the courts in turn curb and regulate the action of the agencies. The result is that the steady thrust of the organizational advance of business and industry is, like a mighty river, channeled, directed, sometimes diverted and sometimes accelerated, but never stopped. It is flowing onward, but where?

For some, probably in the prevailing view of corporate board rooms, this is an impertinent, even dangerous, question. To ask it seems to imply that someone ought to do something about the direction we are taking, but to do this is to invite the disasters that lie in wait for those who attempt to plan the evolution of their society. To attempt an exploratory operation on the Golden Goose might well result in the death of the source of the lovely eggs.

Such an argument has some merit, and to those who understand the workings of our economic system imperfectly (and to greater or lesser degree this includes all of us) it is a cogent argument. But when the argument is pushed to the point of saying, as some indeed do, that we should not even investigate the phenomena of the economic structure that is growing up all around us, we are invited to behave like ostriches who would avoid a possible danger by refusing to look at it. The system has worked well, the argument runs; it has produced the greatest abundance for a large segment of mankind that the world has ever known. Why tamper with it?

Such an attitude is based on an assumption that is contradicted by the contents of this book, for it implies that if no one tampers with the system the conditions that produced our abundance will always remain operative. In these pages we have a factual demonstration that the system that has worked wonders is working one more wonder and changing itself as it grows.

New elements are constantly being introduced which force our economy to modify itself. Technology, for example, presents opportunities which can be exploited only by sophisticated organizations of wealth, managerial expertise, and highly trained scientists and technicians. With these changes generated by technology in methods of production, transportation, and communication come profound changes in the scale of economic enterprise. It is now possible through mass communications media and mass transport to serve nationwide and even world-wide markets. The result is organization of human effort on a scale undreamed of even fifty years ago. Imperceptibly, as the new opportunities of economic advance are seized one by one, a way of life passes and a system of social organization is transmuted. The family business, the individual proprietorship, either ceases to exist or becomes the satellite of the large commercial or financial enterprise. Today upwards of eighty-five percent of Americans who work are employees, and the trend toward organization into group enterprise is still growing at a measurable pace with no logically identifiable stopping place in sight. Even the professions seem about to be invaded by Medicare, group health plans, and the corporate practice of law.

One of the latest phenomena of major impact is the subject of this book. In the stage of institutional development just past, the corporation dominated the economic scene and the individual enterpriser and owner was hull down over the horizon. Now his sails, if he still has any, are also out of sight. The financial institutions are the major influence in corporate stock ownership at present and their influence is growing as individuals become net sellers and the financial institutions buy increasing quantities of shares.

The Baum and Stiles analysis reveals some of the problems that arise when we change the nature of the participants in the economic system without changing the rules of the game. In other words, the legal structure that grounds our economic order is based on the assumption that stockholders in corporations will be individuals seeking to maximize their own gains and protect their rights. But this possibility is negated by the difficulty of shareholders' derivative suits. Furthermore, the new holders of stock voting power seem to be very reluctant to exercise any influence upon corporate management, leaving a gap in the system of checks and balances in the economic system which the law was designed to support. Finally, it appears that the institutions are rapidly reaching a position where they will be locked into the corporations in which they have invested. Their holdings are becoming so large that they cannot easily sell out of a corporation without diminishing the value of an entire issue to the detriment of other shareholders and even themselves.

The tradition of the capitalist market place is, "Every man for himself." But with the economy so tightly knit and with such large amounts of wealth in concentrated holdings this policy could prove very dangerous. The pattern of buying and selling that has prevailed among the institutions in the past shows that they anticipate declines and rises in share prices. More notably, in the few drastic market downturns in recent years at some point the institutions as a group have stepped in to buy heavily, thus halting the plunge in prices. In both these types of activity there is a notable uniformity of behavior among the institutions.

This is only to be expected because the investment imperatives of most of the large institutions are similar; there is rapid, almost instantaneous, communication; and the expertise of these investors is of such a quality that each knows pretty nearly as much as the other. Furthermore, the logic of the investment trade, though it may be an arcane science to the man in the street, runs by fairly definite rules, particularly when one has to operate with the margins of safety required of the institutions who deal in other people's money. It follows, then, that these institutions will reach the same conclusions with regard to a given course of action at a given time. The authors present us with abundant evidence that this is no surmise, but a fact. We need look no further than the overwhelming popularity of certain stock issues among the institutions.

Thus to assume that the financial institutions will act in concert is not to accuse them of collusion. Nevertheless, the net effect of their actions may well be the same as if they had acted collusively. At this point the apologist for the institutions may be heard to say that the institutions, though they may act similarly in a given situation, will never act contrary to the common good, for if they did, they would only be hurting themselves. Until now, as far as we can tell, the institutions have indeed behaved in a manner generally beneficial to the economy. But it is axiomatic that they will continue to do so only as long as it suits their interests or the interests of their clients. After all, they are fiduciaries, so their first loyalty is to their clients. But the point this book raises is that they may well have other responsibilities to the corporations in which they invest and that these duties are not provided for in modern law or business practice.

We have then, the following rather curious state of affairs. The silent partners are very likely to respond in concert in any situation of major significance, like trees bowing before the wind; and since when acting together they have great market power, the impact of their collective action will affect the economy profoundly. And yet, because their collective action is the result of independent choices they have no responsibility for their cumulative effect upon the market and its reverberations throughout the economy. What is true of the market generally is no less true for a particular corporation. Thus, if a group of institutions should decide to leave a corporation to its fate and create heavy selling of its shares by getting out, there is no one to say them nay.

All of this is perhaps merely to say in another way what the authors of this book are pointing out: that the legal and ethical rules designed for another era are not adequate for the present situation. A market populated by elephants treading among pygmies cannot be run by rules designed for competition among equals. Responsibility for behavior ought to be commensurate with power to affect the fortunes of others.

At this point we encounter a serious problem. Should we adopt the position that there shall be no elephants in our market place and seek to reduce the power of the financial institutions? This alternative would seem extremely impractical because, whatever other arguments might be advanced, these institutions are performing a service the American people will not want to be without and we should simply have to frame new institutions to perform the same functions. Should we do nothing? To adopt this position would be to ignore all the problems our authors have discovered.

The solution they suggest is to require the financial institutions to exercise responsible influence upon the corporations in which they hold substantial interests. The institutions, it is argued, are in the position of dominant stockholders and, as such, have a duty to scrutinize the actions of management. Such a solution is probably possible by an extension of legal doctrines already in effect, and an enlightened application of the antitrust laws would probably permit it. But, assuming that these conditions were met, a serious difficulty remains. If the directors of the financial institutions are to become the taskmasters of the corporate officers of industrial enterprises, who is to provide the checks and balances to the power then wielded by the institutions?

However, it is certainly unfair to expect the authors of *The Silent Partners* to answer this question now. Within the scope of the problem they have outlined they have done their job well by pointing up the hitherto unrecognized responsibilities of the financial institutions and identifying one way in which those responsibilities should be met. The institutions, with the power they have at their command, simply cannot, like a small stockholder, buy in and sell out of other corporations without consideration for the other stockholders, and, it may be added, without concern for their impact on the market generally.

To ask how the power of the institutions shall be checked is to indicate the depth and scope of the subject opened up by this book. As the authors point out, the New York Stock Exchange has said that in 1970 the market will be "vastly different" from what it is today. But what will it look like? If the institutions continue to buy shares, will not the market be populated mostly by giants? And if, after 1970, the process continues with institutions buying and not selling, the market will indeed be vastly different; it may not even exist. More likely it will survive as a trading place for the issues of smaller corporations of less interest to the financial institutions and the public. It is tempting to speculate how the functions the market now serves will be carried out then, but that is the subject of another book. It is not the least merit of this one that it invites such speculation—on matters that concern all of us vitally.

PAUL P. HARBRECHT, S.J.

Detroit
July 1965

CONTENTS

1

[decorative greek key pattern]

THE EVOLUTION
OF A PROLETARIAN
CAPITALISM

In 1890 Karl Marx predicted both the centralization of capital and "the conscious technical application of science" to industrial labor.

> That which is now to be expropriated is no longer the labourer working for himself, but the capitalist exploiting many labourers. This expropriation is accomplished by the action of the immanent laws of capitalistic production itself, the centralization of capital. Hand in hand with this centralization, or this expropriation of many capitalists by few, develop, on an ever extending scale, the co-operative form of the labour-process, the conscious technical application of science, the methodical cultivation of the soil, the transformation of the instruments of labour into instruments of labour only usable in common, the economizing of all means of production by their use as the means of production of combined, socialized labour, the entanglement of all peoples in the net of the world-market, and this, the international character of the capitalistic regime.[1]

---

[1] MARX, CAPITAL (Modern Library ed. 1906) at 826.

While the development of capitalism in twentieth-century America has witnessed a kind of centralization of capital, it is a far different variety from that predicted by Marx. Nevertheless, with the accumulation of vast segments of the nation's wealth in the hands of quasi-public institutions and the widespread application of computerized automation, it must now be admitted that the predictions of Marx have been at least partially realized.

What Marx failed to perceive, however, was the inherent potential of capitalism to adapt by democratic processes, and to assume forms much different from the rigid concepts of *laissez faire* economics. Indeed, in mid-twentieth century these words written in 1890 seem unrealistic, if not actually naive:

> Along with the constantly diminishing number of the magnates of capital, who usurp and monopolize all advantages of this process of transformation, grows the mass of misery, oppression, slavery, degradation, exploitation; but with this grows the revolt of the working-class, a class always increasing in numbers, and disciplined, united, organized by the very mechanism of the process of capitalist production itself. The monopoly of capital becomes a fetter upon the mode of production, which has sprung up and flourished along with, and under it. Centralization of the means of production and socialization of labour at last reach a point where they become incompatible with their capitalist integument. This integument is burst asunder. The knell of capitalist private property sounds. The expropriators are expropriated.[2]

That it was a mistake for Marx even to attempt to project the primitive capitalism of 1890 into the twentieth century may now be easy hindsight. But the simple truth is that our "free enterprise" system of today is not the same as it was yesterday. Democratic social reforms have molded the legitimate goals of corporate business into a system more paternalistic, perhaps, than even Marx envisaged. Today we understand and accept rules relating to conditions of employment, imposing maximum hours of work, minimum rates of pay, safe working conditions, and assured income for retired workers.

[2] *Id.* at 826-27.

But what is more important, the worker, indeed the citizenry as a whole, has acquired a vested interest in the corporate goal of return on capital. In twentieth-century United States corporate profit forms the feast in which both labor and capital partake. The proletariat and the bourgeoisie in fact are becoming *one*!

Only a few years ago, in 1959, this nation had an estimated 12.5 million shareholders whose interests were in an average of 3.5 different issues, of which over 68 per cent were listed on the New York Exchange. Today the number of shareholders in American businesses is estimated at nearly 18 million. While the number of direct shareholders, in the words of the Exchange President, represent a kind of "quiet economic revolution that is reshaping America," they do not tell the whole story.

In addition to the 10 per cent of the nation's population that are direct shareholders in American business enterprises, another 60 per cent have indirect equity interests in American business as beneficiaries of pension and retirement funds, as policyholders of insurance companies, as shareholders of investment companies, as beneficiaries of trusts, as settlors or beneficiaries of foundations, as depositors in a variety of savings institutions. Through a complex of institutions that have their genesis in the efforts of a tax-ridden society to adjust its inequities and "promote the general welfare," America has in this century developed its own brand of economic democracy, a kind of proletarian capitalism sometimes euphemistically called a middle-class society. The cynics may say, "You have 70 per cent participation in your capitalistic dream—why not 100 per cent?" To this, one can only answer that the last volley has not been fired and the battle for equal economic security is proceeding at a considerable rate.

The price paid for the mass distribution of wealth in this country is, unfortunately, manifest in bigness that we cannot completely control, complexities we cannot always cope with, and at times conflicting moralities we cannot harmonize. The price of bigness is in turn manifest in the concentration of *control* of the predominant portion of the nation's wealth in the hands of a relatively small number of corporations and individuals. Pretty clearly, the large corporations (in conjunction, some would say, with the large labor unions) dominate the nation's economy. Though few in number, their power and influence vastly overshadow those of the more numerous corporations in the "medium" and "small" categories. The statistics, though familiar, should never be forgotten by those concerned with the concentration of economic power. Of some 100 steel works and rolling mills in the United States, 20 do 85 per cent of the business, 8, approximately 70 per cent, and 4, over 50 per cent. Of some 250 petroleum refining companies, the 20 largest do 84 per cent of the business, the 8 largest, 56 per cent, and the 4 largest, 33 per cent. Out of slightly more than 100 manufacturers of tin cans, the 20 largest do 96 per cent of the business, the 8 largest, 88 per cent, and the 4 largest, 80 per cent. These few facts are illustrative of the pattern that exists throughout the economy. Of 65 industries classified by the Bureau of the Census as having annual shipments in excess of $1 billion, in 26 cases the 8 largest producers controlled over 50 per cent of the business. Of 252 industries with annual shipments between $100 million and $999 million, 112 had more than 50 per cent of their combined production controlled by no more than 8 concerns.[3]

Like it or not, bigness is here to stay; the large corporation is a permanent fixture. The society whose very conception was inspired by the doctrine of *laissez faire* has evolved through a kind of process of natural selection, which seems inherent in the system, into a kind of regulated oligopoly. But whatever the evils of "bigness," it may be this very concentration of power and organization that has provided the affluence which is ours. Yet this is not to say that smaller (and perhaps more efficient) enterprises might not have achieved the same result. Bigness was merely the form that finally evolved to bring the fruits of prosperity to the people. As Professor Berle stated:

> The mid-twentieth century American capitalist system depends on and revolves around the operations of a relatively few very large corporations. It pivots upon industries most of which are concentrated in the hands of extremely few corporate units. Materially, the community has profited mightily. The system of large-scale production and mass distribution carried on by these large institutions can fairly claim the greatest share of

[3] Using statistics supplied by the Bureau of the Census concerning industry in 1954, Senator O'Mahoney submitted testimony on these facts in *Hearings on S. 215 Before the Subcommittee on Antitrust and Monopoly of the Senate Committee on the Judiciary*, 86th Cong., 1st Sess., pt. 11, at 5198-91 (1959).

credit. The face of the country has been changed. Poverty, in the sense that it is understood elsewhere, in America is reduced to minimal proportions.[4]

Inevitably, the social and economic changes reflected in this concentration of power and mass distribution of wealth have altered legal relationships previously thought basic to our jurisprudence, if not to our way of life. The development of the labor movement in the twentieth century and the classic separation of ownership from control resulting from the widespread ownership of American business continue to alter our inherited common-law concepts of private property. The large, publicly held enterprise, employing thousands of persons across the continent, is no longer "private property" in the traditional sense; it has acquired a status vastly different from the country store, with correspondingly different rights and responsibilities. As once stated by the President of Crown Zellerbach Corporation:

> We believe that industry today has acquired a quasi-public character. The days of the industrial tycoon are gone. Corporations are being run by professional managers on behalf of the public owners—the stockholders. Crown Zellerbach started as a family business but has become a public business with some 22,000 share owners. Moreover, a considerable portion of our stock is held by insurance companies, pension funds, and personal and investment trusts . . . so that we are owned by, and responsible to millions of people.[5]

SHAREHOLDER DEMOCRACY AND THE CORPORATE POWER ELITE

Obligations to worker, public, and shareholder there may be. Yet who will insure adherence to these new corporate responsibilities is quite another matter. The separation of ownership from control is inherent in the corporate system: the business of a corporation is to be managed by its board of directors, not its stockholders. The strategic power position of the "professional managers" of corporations, the ownership of which is diffused, was aptly described by Brandeis and by Berle and Means more than twenty-five years ago. They pointed out then the dangers and anomalies of delivering such

---

[4] BERLE, THE 20TH CENTURY CAPITALIST REVOLUTION 28 (1954).
[5] Crown Zellerbach Corporation, Annual Report for the year 1955.

extensive powers to self-perpetuating managements whose principal qualification for corporate office might be little more than the power to control the proxy machinery. In view of the slavish return of managements' proxies by those stockholders who take the trouble to sign and date a preaddressed, postage-paid electronic punch card, control of the proxy machinery, and the authority to use corporate funds to pay the costs of soliciting proxies, virtually insure the regular reelection of incumbent management. As if this phenomenon were not sufficient to perpetuate managements, good and bad, the rapid rise in institutional holdings in recent years has further served to insulate incumbent managements. Here we find that the institutions themselves have, with amazing consistency, supported the managements of portfolio concerns, avowedly on the theory: "When we buy stocks we buy management; if we don't like management we sell the stocks." The continued ability of institutions to follow this rule as their vast holdings continue to mount is the subject of later chapters.

Institutional holdings of common stocks listed on the New York Stock Exchange have risen from approximately 12 per cent of all stocks listed on the Exchange in 1949 to over 20 per cent at the end of 1963, and the Exchange has estimated that this figure will reach 30 per cent by 1970. Projections by others have placed the figure even higher. In other words, at the present time, taken as a whole, incumbent managements are assured of one-fifth of the outstanding corporate vote, without even the need for soliciting a proxy. Control of the vast majority of the nation's wealth is thus removed yet another step from its owners. For, in addition to the diffusion of ownership of 80 per cent of the nation's business among 18 million individual shareholders, the remaining 20 per cent (soon to be 30 per cent) is held by institutions that are themselves vast organizations being run by professional managers for the benefit of an ownership that is equally widely diffused.

As the ownership of the nation's wealth becomes ever more widely distributed, the power to control this wealth becomes increasingly concentrated. Whether this is the result of small shareholder apathy or of the simple fact that a million shareholders cannot, in the nature of things, operate a giant industrial enterprise (or anything else, for that matter), is irrelevant. The fact remains that the mere possession of economic power by the professional managers does not of itself endow them with the requisite ability—not to mention the desired morality—to determine the economic fortunes of 190 million Americans. The situation cannot help but cause thoughtful men to search for means of insuring the responsibility of corporate managers.

This is not to say that the prevailing mode of corporate morality is not superior to what it was a generation ago. The days of the Robber Barons are gone, it is hoped, for good. The vast majority of professional managers are undoubtedly faithful to the responsibilities imposed by their stewardship. The reasons for the improved climate of corporate morality are many, but in large part they are probably traceable to (1) the relatively recent adoption of social and economic legislation and, in particular, the disclosure philosophy embodied in the Securities Act of 1933 and the Securities Exchange Act of 1934; (2) the notable success of the Securities and Exchange Commission in administering these statutes in general and, especially, its leadership in the development of nationally accepted standards of accounting practice that are the highest in the world; (3) the increasing social-mindedness of the bar, together with the heightened participation of lawyers in the daily problems of corporate management; (4) the rising standards of the New York Stock Exchange and other leading exchanges, particularly with respect to problems of conflicts of interest among managements of listed companies; and (5) the maturation of labor unions as a force to be reckoned with by the most powerful of corporate managers.

But the need for checks on management responsibility is still present. The sad results of unlimited management discretion reposed in irresponsible hands are all too common. The literature of recent years is rich with examples of the most flagrant abuses of the public trust. Readers will recall how in 1957 twenty-six-year-old Earl Bell fled to Brazil with, reputedly, $1 million of the funds of Cornucopia Gold Mines, Inc., a publicly held company. The corporate manipulations of Lowell M. Birrell, once in control of Swan Finch Oil Company and Doe Skin Products, will be well remembered by their shareholders. And more recently, the check-writing authority given to socialite Edward Gilbert by the directors of E. L. Bruce Company proved costly for its shareholders, as well as Mr. Gilbert.

Lest the impression be given that the misfortunes that sometimes accompany unfettered management are limited to small or medium-size industry, consider the Chrysler Corporation story of 1960, "perhaps the most celebrated nongovernmental conflicts of interest case in recent years." William C. Newberg was the newly elected president of Chrysler. Soon afterward it was discovered that he

> had previously owned a financial interest in two supplier companies selling parts and materials to Chrysler. Stockholders' suits were filed and a general public uproar followed. The Senate Banking and Currency Committee announced plans to investigate conflicts of interest in top-level management, and the Securities and Exchange Commission threatened to revise its rules so as to require that proxy statements include a full disclosure of the outside interests of executives. Alarmed at the public reaction, the Chrysler Corporation demanded Newberg's resignation and ordered a complete investigation and audit of possible conflicts of interest throughout the corporate management.
>
> Although the investigation cleared Newberg and other top Chrysler executives of any taint of a conflict of interest and there was, in fact, evidence that the two supplier companies in question had actually saved Chrysler money on the purchase of the parts they had supplied, the Chrysler Corporation brought suit to recover all profits made by the two suppliers. A settlement was reached in this action under which Chrysler was paid 450,000 dollars, representing the profits made on sales to it. Mr. Newberg at forty-nine years of age and after twenty-seven years with Chrysler, thereafter found himself thoroughly ostracized by the automotive industry, a result which many observers felt was unduly harsh under the circumstances.[6]

Nevertheless, the comeback that followed for Chrysler must be termed unusual in the annals of American business, as Chrysler earned over $161 million in 1963, and the price of its common stock, twice split two for one, reached a high of $49 per share on the split shares in 1963.

The record demonstrates the continuing need for management checks, for the stakes are enormous, the temptation is great, and

[6] Johnston & Dudley, *Conflicts of Interest in Business and Industry*, 24 Fed. B.J. 344, 345-56 (1964).

man is fallible. How these restraints can be imposed in the context of our present economic system may be one of the crucial questions of our times. In legal theory the primary restraint on management discretion lies with the shareholders. Reality, however, attests to its limited value. The great majority of shareholders do not check management; they endorse it uniformly, whether good, bad, or indifferent. Of course, the power represented by the shareholder vote is not the only check on corporate management. If it were, the days of corporate plundering might still be very much with us. Happily, there are others—nonlegal as well as legal.

Where competition exists, as it does throughout most of the economy, the desire to excel undoubtedly serves to prevent corporate abuse. There is the urge to be first, to be biggest, to outsell a rival, to move one notch higher on the monthly production or sales rating. While the effect of this attitude cannot be measured, few can question its vigorous presence. And, more often than not, the motivation to excel is consistent with the interests of the shareholders, for dedication to corporate goals, at the very least, minimizes opportunity for waste and selfish gain.

The element of competition is sometimes absent, however. Yet there may still remain a force demanding the same results. Some may characterize this drive simply as the desire to do a good job. The president of Standard Oil of New Jersey said:

> We have a stewardship in a company like Jersey Standard and a personal pride. We would like to leave the company in a sounder and more assured position than when we took it over. We are not looking to the company just to support us; we want to make it healthy for future generations and for the employees who will come along. We like to feel that it is a good place for people to work. We have equal responsibilities to other groups: stockholders, customers, and the public generally, including government. What is the proper balance for the claims of these different sections? What part of the profits should go to stockholders? What part to employees' wages? What part to the customer in lower prices and improved quality? Keeping the proper balance in these things is one of the most important matters that corporate management has to consider. We hope that we learn more about them (and each generation of man-

agement that comes in has to learn them); we are making some progress toward responsible direction.[7]

Fear may also spark the drive to excel, to do a good job: fear of public scorn, fear of possible congressional investigation or other governmental action and, probably most of all, fear of a shareholder's derivative suit. The effect of these fears as a check on corporate management has been greatly augmented by the reporting and disclosure provisions of the Securities Exchange Act of 1934[8] and the related rules of the Securities and Exchange Commission. The statutory requirement of full disclosure makes the facts available to institutions and interested shareholders. Thus, companies whose securities are listed on a national securities exchange, and other companies subject to the jurisdiction of the 1934 act, must periodically disclose in reports to the SEC (reports that become public record) important corporate developments, including such matters as changes in corporate control, material acquisitions or dispositions of assets or securities, as well as any matters recently submitted to a vote of security holders. In addition they must file annual financial statements, conforming to the Commission's accounting requirements and certified by *independent* public accountants, together with unaudited interim statements at midyear. Companies soliciting proxies must reveal, among other things, the details of management stock options plans, the amount of compensation paid to officers and directors in excess of thirty thousand dollars a year, and all material interests of management personnel in transactions with their companies. Officers and directors and more-than-10-per-cent shareholders must report their purchases and sales of equity securities issued by their companies. As later discussed, profits from "short-swing" trading in such securities are recoverable in a suit by any shareholder on behalf of the corporation.

Whatever the fears of corporate management may have been before, every corporate lawyer today is familiar with the client's call seeking advice as to whether a particular transaction, if engaged in, will have to be reported to the Commission; and he knows, too, how often perfectly legal transactions are avoided, if they have any

---

[7] MAURER, GREAT ENTERPRISES—GROWTH AND BEHAVIOR OF THE BIG CORPORATION 75-76 (1955).

[8] Sections 13 and 15; 15 U.S.C. §§ 78m and 78o.

appearance of evil, simply because they would have to be so re-ported. Moreover, in response to the SEC's *Special Study of the Securities Markets,* Congress enacted legislation in 1964 that makes the reporting and proxy-soliciting requirements applicable to the bulk of publicly owned companies that are not listed on a securities exchange but are traded over-the-counter.

The problem of providing adequate checks on corporate management is often likened to the problem of causing the elected to be responsive to the electorate in a political democracy. This analogy persists because the evolution of the corporate form has been deeply affected by our political history. In the body politic of a populous nation, the most the citizens can do is approve, from time to time, a slate of candidates as their leaders and occasionally pass on a referendum that affects them directly. In the very large corporations, with hundreds of thousands of shareholders, the shareholders' rights are very much the same. But, even more than the political franchise, the shareholders' rights go unexercised and the corporate process becomes "democratic" in form but not in substance. There are several reasons dictating this conclusion. For one, the corporate democracy operates as a "one-party system." Management, not the shareholders, selects a single slate of candidates and controls the proxy machinery, not to mention the corporate coffers for campaign funds. The "choice" offered to the shareholder is illusory. There are no alternative candidates to receive his votes. Of course, there is a remedy available to him which is not so readily available to the political citizen: the shareholder can leave his economic "country"; he can sell if he chooses and move to another corporation. But obviously the exercise of this "right" does not go far toward encouraging shareholder democracy. On the contrary, it can fairly be assumed that it has the opposite effect, and for those "locked in" with large capital gains, even this alternative may not be available.

Moreover, the complexity of modern corporate affairs and the difficulty of obtaining and analyzing complex financial and scientific data undoubtedly contribute to shareholder apathy. While the same problem exists, in somewhat different context, for the citizens of a body politic, opposing political candidates normally *do* offer alternative programs in such matters as foreign aid, agricultural subsidies, welfare, and civil rights, about which most of us have, at the very least, some predispositions. The voter has an awareness of the state of the nation: he knows whether he pays high taxes, whether the economy is prosperous, and whether his country is at peace. The corporate citizen, on the other hand, can look to his company's earnings and to his dividends, but he is, by and large, ill equipped to judge the soundness of corporate policies. How can he do more than ratify, for the convenience of management (or for their protection from possible derivative suits), those proposals submitted for vote, such as ratification of a stock option plan, modification of an indenture provision to permit additional corporate borrowing or, perhaps, an amendment to the by-laws indemnifying the company's officers and directors? These matters may well be significant to the corporation, but they are not likely to cause the average shareholder to lose much sleep. At managements' recommendation he will return his proxy marked "For" because, in effect, he has no other rational choice.

This is not to say that corporate managements are at all disheartened by lack of shareholder interest. On the contrary, they are delighted and may look upon the occasional inquisitive shareholder as a menace, a potential troublemaker, or a crank. In fact, this same attitude would, and sometimes does, embrace the inquiries of institutional investors as well, except for the nagging fear that the institutions might avoid the corporation's stock and perhaps depress its market price, a risk management would rather not take, for it cuts at the heart of the stock option plan.

The fragmentation of shareholder vote, coupled with management domination of the proxy machinery, places self-perpetuating power in the hands of entrenched leadership. And this condition is heightened when we recall that majority ownership of the large publicly held corporations is a near impossibility. As a rule, no individual shareholder holds more than 1 per cent of the outstanding stock. And even institutional holdings generally do not exceed 5 per cent. Of the five largest issues of common stocks listed on the New York Stock Exchange, each with aggregate market values of between $10 billion and $30 billion at the end of 1962, the Exchange found that the aggregate amount of such issues held by eighteen hundred institutions was only 4.5 per cent of the total amount outstanding.

Thus, challenge to management comes only from the occasional shareholder or group of shareholders who together possess a relatively substantial minority position that can serve as a base to offset the advantage inherent in management's position. By way of example, John D. Rockefeller, Jr., assumed that his 14.9 per cent stock ownership in Standard Oil Company of Indiana assured him absolute working control, which he exercised for many years through Colonel Stewart, the chairman of the board. When Mr. Rockefeller decided to rid himself of Stewart, the Colonel resisted. The proxy fight that ensued was no easy victory for Mr. Rockefeller. He was able to muster only 59 per cent of the vote, and that at tremendous cost.

The reality of minority control has long been recognized by statute. Both the Investment Company Act of 1940 and the Public Utility Holding Company Act of 1935 provide for presumption of control when one person is the beneficial owner of 25 per cent or 10 per cent, respectively, of a company's voting securities. And, for purposes of Section 16 of the Securities Exchange Act of 1934, 10-per-cent shareholders, along with officers and directors, are arbitrarily deemed "insiders" who must file reports relating to their ownership of, and transactions in, the equity securities of their companies. The profits realized by insiders from purchases and sales or sales and purchases of such securities, within a six-month period, are recoverable in a suit by the corporation, irrespective of whether the officer, director, or shareholder actually had access to or used "inside information." If the corporation refuses to bring suit, any shareholder may do so on behalf of the corporation, and the courts have permitted generous allowances for attorneys' fees and expenses to encourage effective enforcement of the policy of the Act.

Similarly, the disclosure requirements of the Securities Act of 1933 are applicable to public distributions of securities on behalf of controlling persons, as well as issuers. The courts and the SEC have held the requirements of that statute applicable to persons owning far less than a majority of the outstanding stock. In this context the SEC believes that every corporation, with rare exception, is "controlled" by an identifiable individual or group of persons.

When viewed in the light of (1) the diffusion of corporate shareownership, (2) the prevailing mood of small shareholder apathy, and (3) the historical statutory recognition of minority control, the vast holdings of institutions take on implications that may not be readily apparent when such holdings are simply stated as a percentage of outstanding shares. The possibility begins to emerge that these holdings may represent still another potential check on corporate management that as yet remains substantially untapped.

SOME EXISTING RESTRAINTS ON THE CORPORATE POWER ELITE

The Corporate Democrats. In the face of what would seem to be rather astounding obstacles, there are those who cling to the belief that the ultimate maturation of a true shareholder democracy remains, in the last analysis, the surest and best check on the fidelity of corporate management. The most vocal leaders of this movement have been Lewis Gilbert, assisted by his brother John, and Mrs. Wilma Soss, president of the Federation of Women Shareholders in American Business, Inc. Mr. Gilbert has visualized the goals of his movement as

> advocating every American a shareholder with a vote, a voice and a stake in the democratic management of the country's corporations . . . fighting for the greatest profit, preferably in the form of dividends, for the greatest number of American people . . . fighting for a people's democratic capitalism in which 70,000,000 Americans, instead of the present 7,500,000 will own and operate American business as its stockholders, supplying both capital and brains through the functioning of corporate democracy.[9]

The principal planks in the Corporate Democrats' platform are: (1) cumulative voting for the election of directors to permit minority representation on the board, (2) elimination of the stagger system of electing directors—that is, the system of electing only a portion of the board of directors in each year, (3) election of outside—nonmanagement—directors to give the board broader scope, (4) the holding of annual meetings at easily accessible locations, preferably in one of the large cities (many of the larger corporations still hold their annual shareholders' meetings in obscure towns in New Jersey or Delaware), (5) freedom of speech at shareholders' meetings, (6) postmeeting reports, (7) management owner-

[9] GILBERT, DIVIDENDS AND DEMOCRACY 15-16 (1956).

ship of stock, and (8) limitations on executive compensation, current and deferred.

The movement of the Corporate Democrats has been small but loud. The financial press, often hard pressed for colorful news, has found color in the Gilberts and Mrs. Soss. For example, a few years ago Mrs. Soss appeared at the meeting called to approve the merger of the Chemical Corn Exchange Bank and the New York Trust Company. She was wearing all white attire with the exception of a heavy black veil to mourn the "passing" of the Corn Exchange name, which was then being dropped in favor of Chemical Bank New York Trust Company.

In the opinion of some corporate managers, the stated goals of the Gilbert group represent incredible naivete, and others would go so far as to question the good faith of the "professional Corporate Democrats." Nevertheless, publicity can sometimes bring results. In an interview with one of the authors, Lewis Gilbert produced a letter from a corporate president that stated that the company, in general, would accept Mr. Gilbert's suggestion that board meetings be held monthly instead of quarterly. In the same interview Mr. Gilbert plucked another letter from a huge pile of current correspondence, this one from the public relations manager of another large corporation, addressed to Mr. Gilbert's brother John. It stated that the company hoped to broaden its activities in encouraging shareholder attendance at corporate meetings. The impact of Gilbert's persistent prodding can be found by reading many corporations' annual reports. Commenting on its 1959 annual meeting, the board chairman of the American Machine & Foundry Company stated in the company's postmeeting report:

> Highlights of our 59th annual meeting of stockholders . . . were broadcast over a National Broadcasting Company coast-to-coast radio net work the same evening.
>
> This unusual nationwide projection of our meeting, the first of its kind in industrial and radio history, enabled thousands of our stockholders, employees, and the general public to hear portions of the on-the-spot proceedings.

The focal point of the Corporate Democrat's activities is the annual meeting of shareholders. His principal weapon in the battle to influence management is the question from the floor, since he can seldom if ever muster sufficient votes for adoption of specific proposals not supported by management. Mr. Gilbert, for example, will go to great lengths to ask his questions, and if management attempts to deny him this right, he will broadcast the fact to the world. Needless to say, the inordinate amount of press coverage received by the Corporate Democrats works to their advantage in this respect.

Effectiveness of a Corporate Democrat at the annual meeting requires studious preparation. His question must be carefully chosen and appropriately framed; it must be precise, specific and founded on fact. If his question is too broad, such as "Why doesn't the corporation pay a higher dividend?" management can easily respond with a facile generalization to the effect that they have used their best judgment as to the proper balance of competing demands on the corporation's funds. Such a reply may well be true, but it does not accomplish the Corporate Democrat's purpose.

Framing a narrow yet startling question that can be properly raised at an annual meeting may not be easy. The shareholder must be familiar with corporate affairs. He must know the company's weaknesses and management's mistakes, and such information may be hard to grasp. The reports required by the SEC are comprehensive, but their reading often requires a talent comparable to that which went into their drafting. This the untutored lay shareholder may not have. Mr. Gilbert once wrote, "One of the chief things I learned early in my career was the necessity for sound and accurate information on the affairs of each corporation whose annual meeting I attend."[10] Those who have followed Mr. Gilbert's activities know that he learned this lesson well, for he is usually well armed with the facts.

To wage his campaign Mr. Gilbert has gathered around him a group able to devote a substantial amount of time to the cause of Corporate Democracy. In time, Mr. Gilbert has suggested, these allies may form a single organization. Each year, from June to January, the Gilbert group reviews and plans for the annual meetings scheduled for the following six months. If possible, he and his fellow Corporate Democrats will use the Securities and Exchange Commission's Shareholder Proposal Rule, which permits any share-

[10] *Id.* at 37.

holder (regardless of the number of shares held) to compel management to publish his proposal and a hundred-word supporting statement in the corporation's proxy statement.[11] All the SEC requires is that the proposal be appropriate for shareholder action under the applicable state corporation law and that the hundred-word supporting statement be truthful and not misleading. The proposal and the supporting statement must first be reviewed, together with the rest of the proxy statement, by the SEC staff. The same rules allow management to respond with a hundred-word counterstatement.

But, for the Corporate Democrats, the shareholder proposal is usually a one-time-only affair. Under the rules, if the shareholder's petition is rejected it may not be resubmitted for three years, unless 3 per cent of the votes were initially cast in its favor. In order for a proposal to be resubmitted a second time it must have received 6 per cent of the vote and, for a third presentation, 10 per cent. In almost any large corporation, the initial 3 per cent requirement forms an effective barrier.

The Proxy Fight. At first glance, it might seem that a significant opportunity for stockholder restraint on management discretion would be the proxy fight or the threat of one. After all, loss of control by top management often would mean loss of a job. Hence, when an individual or group of shareholders appears to be gathering control of substantial voting power, management understandably prepares to fight for its very survival. Emotions can reach sharp peaks and, despite the restraining efforts of the SEC, a volley of epithets frequently ensues. Surely, the conflagration ought to provide the small independent shareholders, including the Corporate Democrats, the chance to make their influence felt. In fact, however, this has not been the result of corporate proxy struggles. No doubt one of the principal reasons for this was cited by Professor Berle:

> The directors of General Electric are, I should think, far more likely to choose a good slate of directors than would be a committee of small stockholders. Indeed, on the relatively rare occasions when a "democratic" contest for shareholders' votes has taken place, through a campaign to secure proxies, one is

[11] Rule 14a-8, 17 CFR 240.14a-8 adopted by the Securities and Exchange Commission pursuant to § 14 of the Securities Exchange Act of 1934, 15 U.S.C. 78n.

struck with the fact that the campaigners rarely discuss the real issues, probably because they are too complex for easy understanding.[12]

The 1954 contest for control of the New York Central Railroad provides a case in point. On the floor of the 1954 annual meeting, the late Mr. Robert R. Young, the man who challenged the Central management, supported the independent request of a Corporate Democrat for cumulative voting. The next year, after Young had defeated the management, he voted against the proposal, which would have allowed the old management, which still represented a very substantial minority, to regain a voice in the corporation. Young impliedly promised to pay the costs of the proxy contest from his own account, and not that of the Central. This, too, was later repudiated when he succeeded in gaining control of the Central.

Candidates in proxy contests offer the stockholders a great deal, much as opposing political candidates offer the citizenry a great deal. Both need votes. For example, in 1956, insurgents defeated Perry Selheimer of the Norfolk & Southern Railroad by a vote of 182,339 shares to 176,480. After his defeat, in a bid for reelection, Mr. Selheimer promised the Corporate Democrats much, and Gilbert, for one, agreed to switch his vote.

Where the political citizen as a matter of course may check his elected official by choosing between two different major parties at the next regular election, only in the rare case of a proxy fight is the corporate shareholder given the benefits of a two-party system as a check on management. But the workings of the democratic process seem less attuned to the problems of corporate complexities. The proxy fight cannot be equated to an institutionalized two-party political system. For the small shareholder the proxy fight is of limited value. He cannot even feel as confident as the political citizen that the man he is voting to throw out is less capable than the man he is voting in. Said the financial writer, J. A. Livingston:

> [A] proxy battle is just another political campaign. And stockholders, like voters, choose only as well as their knowledge of the men and the issues permits, which, considering that most

[12] BERLE, POWER WITHOUT PROPERTY 108-09 (1959).

stockholders are too busy with their own affairs and careers, is usually superficial. Only when the professionals, the institutions, get into a proxy fight is there knowledge and understanding in depth. And proxy battles . . . is what the professionals do not get into: That is the great gap in stockholder potency.[13]

Only in the brief period from 1953 to 1956 did the logic that militates against the proxy fight give way. More than twenty substantial corporations were then challenged annually, to what must have been the deep concern of top management generally. But in 1957 reason seemed to reassert itself; the number of contests dropped to twelve. Thereafter, a further decline resulted until the years 1960-1964 witnessed an average of but five proxy fights annually.

Quantitatively, the statistics bear out the conclusion already stated: the proxy fight, like total war, occurs infrequently. Yet it must be added that war *can* be declared, even upon the giant corporation. In 1962 the Murcheson brothers staged a colossal fight to wrest management of Allegheney Corporation from Allen P. Kirby, but a year later Kirby once again regained control.

Except for the occasional cataclysm—for that is how one must describe a war to win control of the modern corporation—the scene has been relatively quiet in recent years. The dominant reason for this apparent state of corporate tranquility probably can be found in the very steep cost that a challenger must be prepared to bear. Some have estimated that a battle for a large corporation would cost the contestants approximately $143,000 to $215,000, and the incumbent management $175,000 to $300,000. Even these figures are probably much too conservative. The costs in the Murcheson-Kirby fight were estimated to have run into the millions, although concededly this may not be a typical case. As the high costs of a proxy war lead to fewer such battles and more compromises of the few that are started, the shareholder will find this check further limited. Even if a struggle should occur, incumbent management need not fear total ouster. It may be able to compromise by allowing minority representation on the board, thus conceding nothing the minority might not achieve if the corporation elected its directors by cumula-

[13] LIVINGSTON, THE AMERICAN STOCKHOLDER 150 (1958).

tive voting. In any event, and irrespective of which side prevails, the corporation—and thus ultimately the shareholders—pays the costs.

The Derivative Suit. What then is there to check corporate management? In the United States the only legal check, aside from the vote, is the derivative suit. Briefly, this is an action brought in the name of the corporation, to redress any wrong that the corporation *could* have sued to redress.[14] Of course, the shareholder's right to bring such an action stems from the fact that management will be understandably loath to institute proceedings against itself for misconduct. If the corporation has been injured by mismanagement or abuse of position that does not fall within the realm of activities protected by the so-called business judgment rule, any shareholder at the time of the injury may sue on behalf of the corporation. Thus the scope of the derivative suit is confined to wrongs that are so flagrant that the board could not ratify the questionable conduct by a valid exercise of its business judgment. Within this area the derivative suit is a potent weapon for righting corporate wrongs, despite the fact that it has, over the years, been subjected to some rather severe limitations.

The career of Clarence H. Venner provides a starting point for understanding the derivative suit and a reason for the strictures imposed. It was the profession of Mr. Venner to sue those corporate leaders who he thought had forgotten the principle that directors and officers stand in a fiduciary relationship to the corporation and are accountable to it for failure to discharge their duties in good faith and with care.[15] Among those brought to the bench by the not so venerable Mr. Venner were the directors of Atchison, Topeka and Santa Fe Railway, Union Pacific Railroad, Great Northern Railway, Pullman Palace Car Company, United States Steel Corporation, J. P. Morgan & Company, New York Central Railroad, Guaranty Trust Company, Bethlehem Steel Corporation, New York Life Insurance Company, and American Telephone and Telegraph Company—a distinguished list by any standards. While the direct awards resulting from trial went to the corporate treasury, Venner

---

[14] Continental Securities Co. v. Belmont, 99 N.E. 138 (N.Y. 1912).

[15] Twin-Lick Oil Co. v. Marbury, 91 U.S. 587 (1875); Pepper v. Litton, 308 U.S. 295 (1939); Briggs v. Spaulding, 141 U.S. 132 (1891); Kavanaugh v. Gould, 119 N.E. 237 (N.Y. 1918).

was still able to earn a handsome personal profit: "He settled a
suit against the Great Northern by selling Hill, its doughty president and no pushover, 980 shares of stock, for $513,000. Venner had
paid $188,587 for the shares. He received $300,000 for bonds with
a, face value of $30,000 by withdrawing a suit against Union
Pacific."[16]

The label attached to Venner, of course, is the now well-known
"strike suitor." The term refers to one who brings a complaint in
bad faith to force a settlement disproportionate to the plaintiff's
interests and without any real desire to effect a recovery for the
benefit of all of the shareholders. In defense of such a charge Venner
is reported to have answered:

> I have a large investment to protect, and it is a bad thing to
> permit a large corporation to jam through plans involving
> millions. You see, the average stockholder's proxy means
> nothing. He sends it in slavishly at the call of his directors. . . .
> I am not a stockholder of this kind. I make it my business to
> be informed and I conceive it to be my duty not only to protect
> my own interests but those of unthinking minority security
> owners.[17]

Of the intense feeling generated by the bringing of a derivative suit,
one author wrote:

> The opprobrium which may be heaped upon the plaintiff and
> counsel in a stockholder's action, by lawyers who have other-
> wise a reputation for calmness, courtesy and fairness, would be
> unbelievable if so many examples were not recorded in stenog-
> raphers' minutes and printed briefs.
>
> The following from the brief in a recent New York case, is
> a fairly mild sample: "This is a champertous, unlawful suit,
> which should not be countenanced by this Court of Equity.
> The original plaintiff's . . . stock was put in his name by his
> then attorneys for the sole purpose of instigating strike litiga-
> tion. . . . Plaintiff . . . was also brought into this case by his
> lawyer, from whom he received all his information. . . . The
> case is patently one instituted and fostered by lawyers for the

---

[16] LIVINGSTON, THE AMERICAN STOCKHOLDER 50 (1958).
[17] *Id.* at 52.

sole purpose of getting a fee for themselves; it is of such un-
savory origin that no Court of Equity should entertain it. . . .
The plaintiffs in this case, holding trivial stock interests, are
obviously motivated solely by a sinister, self-seeking purpose."

The viciousness of such attacks militates against their very
purpose; it insures that stockholders' suits will be instituted
and conducted, as a rule, only by those who are impervious
to abuse—and hence capable of the most objectionable conduct.[18]

Right or wrong the clamor against the "strike suit" resulted in
the imposition of judicial and legislative restrictions on its successful
institution. Among the most widely known of these hurdles is the
security-for-expenses statute. In New York the law requires the court
to set a bond to be posted by the plaintiff unless he holds a beneficial
interest in 5 per cent, or $50,000's worth, of the corporation's stock.
The defendant must request the court to impose the bond.[19] In his
memorandum on the security statute, which was enacted in 1944,
the Governor of New York wrote, in part:

There are many classes of action in this State and in other
states where the party must put up security for costs. It has
frequently been suggested in this State that no action should
be brought except upon the putting up of security for costs.
This particular bill affects only one kind of action which has
been the subject of great abuse and malodorous scandal.

· · · · ·

In the cases requiring security, the amount is left to the
discretion of the court. This would be substantially the same
court which now has the power in that kind of action to impose payment of counsel fees upon the unsuccessful defendant.
It would seem that if the court could be trusted for the one
purpose, it could be trusted for the other.

Soon after the law was enacted in New York, Professor Hornstein wrote:

Simply stated, the law—insofar as it concerns a publicly owned

---

[18] Berlack, *Stockholders' Suits: A Possible Substitute,* 35 MICH. L. REV. 597,
605, 606 (1937).
[19] N.Y. Bus. Corp. Law § 627.

corporation—bars stockholders from maintaining a derivative suit on its behalf unless they are the holders of stock having a market value of more than $50,000. The apparent alternatives are mere camouflage.[20]

The statute did not rid the courts of the derivative suitor; he persisted, trying to mitigate the stringent provisions of the law. In *Baker v. MacFadden Publications, Inc.,*[21] the plaintiff, owning only four-thousandths of 1 per cent of the corporation's stock, having a market value of $350, attempted to avoid the security bond by obtaining a list of other shareholders who might have wanted to join in the suit. The court denied the plaintiff the right to examine the corporate books for the purpose of obtaining the list (two justices dissenting). The New York statute has recently been changed to make it clear that the plaintiff must now be the *beneficial owner* of 5 per cent or $50,000's worth of the corporation's stock.

Even where the derivative suitor has succeeded in overcoming the burden of the expense statute, he may meet court-imposed difficulties almost as great as those instituted by the legislature. For example, there is the judicial rule that a demand must be made upon the shareholders to bring suit before a derivative action may commence. In some cases this demand must be made although the corporation is held by thousands of stockholders, or even when the stockholders could not validly ratify the action by any kind of vote.[22] The origin of the demand requirement springs from the

[20] Hornstein, *The Death Knell of Stockholders' Derivative Suits in New York,* 32 CALIF. L. REV. 123, 124 (1944). The new law was not received particularly well by the courts. Thus, although the trial court in Shielcrawt v. Moffet, 49 N.Y.S. 2d 64, 72, *aff'd,* 51 N.Y.S. 2d 188 (1944), *rev'd on other grounds,* 61 N.E.2d 435 (N.Y. 1945), upheld the constitutionality of § 61(b) (the predecessor to § 627) it also stated: "The stockholder's access to the courts is thus made dependent on the magnitude of his till. The statute contrives a new alloy as a criterion in stockholder's grievances." See also 62 HARV. L. REV. 309, 319 (1948).

Somewhat surprisingly, the civil liability provisions of both the Securities Act of 1933 (§ 11(e)) and the Securities Exchange Act of 1934 (§ 18a) permit the court, in its discretion, to require security for reasonable expenses, including attorney's fees. The provisions have seldom been invoked in securities litigation.

[21] 59 N.Y.S. 2d 841 (1946).

[22] Pomerantz v. Clark, 101 F. Supp. 341 (D. Mass. 1951); S. Solomont & Sons Trust, Inc. v. New England Theatres Operating Corporation, 93 N.E.2d 241 (Mass. 1950).

English decision in *Foss v. Harbottle*,[23] where the court reasoned it was necessary first to allow the other shareholders an opportunity to act, thus preventing what might prove to be useless action by the court. Today the requirement serves other purposes:

> Demand is usually justified as being instrumental in preventing vexatious suits against the corporation, encouraging settlement of problems within the corporation, and permitting management to make rapid and authoritative decisions without being harassed by the dissenting minority.[24]

Most courts agree that where the directors are the wrongdoers, it would be futile to ask them to bring suit against themselves, and in New York the statute simply requires the plaintiff to describe what effort has been made to cause the corporation to litigate, or to state the reasons why such effort has not been made.[25] There are those who believe that the courts have thus equalled the legislature in halting the derivative suit.

But the most effective bar to such suits comes neither from the legislature nor the judiciary but from the shareholder's inability to discover a wrong and, once it is discovered, to prove it.

> It is probably no exaggeration to say that in many cases the transactions are so complicated that even skilled accountants and attorneys, informed that the corporation has been abused, find it impossible to unravel the intricacies and discover the nature of the wrong before suit is barred by the statute of limitations.[26]

The difficulty of proof confronting the shareholder wishing to bring a derivative action is one that arises at the inception. In *Price v. Standard Oil Co.*, the court stated:

> Undoubtedly the tendency of the courts of this state in recent years has been to insist more rigorously on the requirement that in a derivative stockholder's suit, facts, rather than con-

[23] 67 Eng. Rep. 189 (1843).
[24] 55 MICH. L. REV. 450, 451-52 (1957).
[25] N.Y. Bus. Corp. Law § 626(c).
[26] Hornstein, *Legal Controls for Intracorporate Abuse—Present and Future*, 41 COLUM. L. REV. 405, 420 (1941).

clusory assertions, characterizations, and charges, must be set forth in the complaint.[27]

As *Price* indicates, the courts have not helped to ease the plaintiff's burden for fear of stimulating the "strike suit." Today, in all fairness, this attitude is largely unwarranted. Much of the personal profit has been taken from the plaintiff. Proceeds from even an unapproved court settlement before trial are quite properly impressed with a trust for the benefit of the corporation's other shareholders. The court held in *Clarke v. Greenberg:*

> Requiring an accounting for moneys received in a private settlement introduces no new element. It simply amounts to a logical application of a fundamental principle inherent in the representative relation. When one assumes to act for another, regardless of the manner or method used in accomplishing a successful termination, he should willingly account for his stewardship. The plaintiff-stockholder, in good conscience, should not be allowed to retain the proceeds of a derivative suit discontinued by stipulation, to his individual use, in opposition to the corporation, any more than the proceeds of a judgment or a settlement with court approval.[28]

In New York this rule is now statutory. Section 626(d) of the Business Corporation Law declares that a shareholder's derivative suit "shall not be discontinued, compromised or settled without the approval of the court having jurisdiction of the action." Further, some courts deny an award for the plaintiff's counsel fees unless there is pecuniary benefit to the corporation.[29]

The vagaries have been alleviated somewhat in New York. Statute allows the plaintiff, at the discretion of the court, expenses and attorney fees if he has been partially successful. But the same statute makes it clear that an accounting must be made to the corporation for all other proceeds arising from the case.[30] That the derivative suit should be subjected to at least reasonable limitations

[27] 55 N.Y.S. 2d 891, 893 (1945).

[28] 71 N.E.2d 443 (N.Y. 1947).

[29] Eisenberg v. Central Zone Property Corp., 116 N.Y.S. 2d 154 (1952), rev'd, 118 N.Y.S. 2d 919 (1953).

[30] N.Y. Bus. Corp. Law § 626(e).

should not be too surprising. After all, corporate laws are, for the most part, written by corporate lawyers—who are not a dull group when it comes to protecting their clients' interest. Professor Hornstein has written:

> It must not be forgotten that the frequent disclosure of corporate scandals testifies to the inadequacy of the stockholder's suit as a means of keeping corporate stewards honest. But until the stockholder's suit is supplemented with an effective preventive device such as applications of criminal sanctions, the suit is society's principal safeguard.[31]

The derivative suit remains the single most effective restraint on abuse of trust by corporate management. The reporting and disclosure requirements of federal securities legislation and the discovery provisions of the Federal Rules of Civil Procedure[32] have gone a long way toward making the necessary information available to the derivative suitor. Moreover, in recent years the holdings of the courts that violations of federal securities legislation (including the rules of the SEC) give rise to civil remedies which can be enforced derivatively have not only added another string to the suitor's bow, in many cases they have provided a ready cause of action that (1) can be brought in the federal courts where the liberal discovery rules can be employed by the plaintiff; (2) is not subject to the many technical common law defenses; and (3) does not require the stringent standards of proof that would apply to the older common law fraud remedies.[33] These cases are all based on the theory that a violation of the prophylactic provisions of remedial statutes gives rise to a cause of action that sounds essentially in tort, in favor of an injured person in the class intended to have the protection of the statute. Further, under the doctrine of

---

[31] Hornstein, *The Counsel Fee in Stockholder's Derivative Suits*, 39 COLUM. L. REV. 784, 786 (1939); the Federal courts have, in general, taken a more lenient view of the derivative suitor, although the rule in diversity cases may require them to apply state law, including a state's security for expense statute. See Erie Railroad Co. v. Tompkins, 304 U.S. 64 (1937); Cohen v. Beneficial Industrial Loan Corp., 337 U.S. 541 (1949).

[32] FED. R. CIV. P., Part V, Rules 26 through 37.

[33] Kardon v. National Gypsum Co., 69 F. Supp. 512 (E.D. Pa. 1946); Speed v. Transamerica Corp., 71 F. Supp. 457 (D. Del. 1947), 135 F. Supp. 176 (1955), *modified*, 235 F. 2d 369 (3d Cir. 1956).

"pendent jurisdiction," the plaintiff who asserts a *federal* right can, at the same time, try his state-based case in the federal courts if it arose out of the same facts alleged in the federal suit.[34] He may thus gain access to the more liberal federal rules for his state cause of action, even though he fails to perfect his federal claim. This procedural device has proved significant in a number of cases in recent years against the directors and officers of regulated investment companies (discussed in later chapters).

As the ownership of American business becomes increasingly diffuse, it assumes an ever more public character, and the need for workable provisions to insure management fidelity becomes even more acute. It is in this context that the emerging new force—the institutional investor—with an enormous stake in the success of the nation's business, will be viewed. On the one side there is the danger that as the institutional investors grow, control of the nation's productive capacity becomes even further removed from its owners. On the other side there are opportunities springing from the fact that the institutions are rapidly acquiring, and indeed already possess, enormous powers that can be brought to bear to insure management fidelity.

As yet these powers have remained substantially unexercised. The crucial question seems inescapable: Does not the accumulation of economic power carry with it correlative responsibilities? While corporate democracy may well be an unworkable ideal, there may be other means at hand to check on corporate management. The genius of the common law has been its great capacity to respond to what Mr. Justice Holmes described as the "felt necessities of the times." The rising dominance of institutional investors as corporate shareholders may ultimately give rise to shareholder responsibilities hitherto unheard of.

Who, then, are the institutional investors and what is the extent of their power?

[34] Hurn v. Oursler, 289 U.S. 238 (1933).

2

🔲🔲🔲🔲🔲🔲

THE NATURE AND
FUNCTIONS OF
INSTITUTIONAL INVESTORS

The Size and Growth of Institutional Investors

Today much of the nation's privately owned wealth is controlled by banks, insurance companies, savings and loan associations, pension funds, investment companies, college and university endowments, and foundations. These are the institutions we here speak of as "institutional investors." At the end of 1962 total assets of all institutional investors amounted to nearly $695 billion. Commercial banks had assets valued at over $297 billion at the end of 1962; life insurance companies, $133 billion; and noninsured private pension funds, $39 billion. Investment companies had total assets of $29.4 billion, of which $22.9 billion were held by open-end companies ("mutual funds") and $6.5 billion by closed-end companies. (Of the closed-end companies, $3.2 billion, or 49 per cent of their total assets, were held by a single nondiversified company, Christiana Securities Corporation.)

Impressive as these figures are from the standpoint of sheer size, they are somewhat misleading. For they give the impression that the different classes of institutions are wholly separate and removed from each other, perhaps in a line of direct competition.

This is not entirely so. Pension trusts are managed by banks, under trust instruments that give them wide investment discretion. In 1955 Father Harbrecht found that thirteen New York banks managed three-fifths of all pension fund assets. The New York Stock Exchange recently estimated that three-fourths of all private noninsured pension funds are managed by banks, and on the basis of the year-end 1962 figures, this would represent assets of approximately $29 billion. From the standpoint of *control*, then, the total asset figure for commercial banks should be $326 billion instead of $297 billion. To this should be added $98 billion in savings and time deposits held by commercial banks, and personal trust funds that in 1960 were estimated at $62 billion. Commercial banks, therefore, own or control assets valued at nearly $500 billion, nearly four times as much as the next largest type of institution and more than all other institutions combined.

Hence, the assets owned or controlled by commercial banks alone approximated the Gross National Product in 1962—$554.8 billion—and exceeded the public debt, which was $421.2 billion. Total assets of all institutions—$695 billion—compare with total public and private debt at year-end 1962 of $1,176.4 billion.

The importance of institutional investors to the American people can hardly be exaggerated. Nearly every individual, especially if employed, today relies in one way or another on investment institutions. He may be the beneficiary of a corporate pension or profit-sharing plan where he works; he may have purchased his home with a mortgage from a savings and loan association, in which case his home will be insured by a fire and casualty insurance company; he may have a savings account with a local savings bank as well as a checking account with a commercial bank; he may have life insurance to protect his family; and if he has funds left over after meeting the family's regular expenses, he may be buying shares of a mutual fund, perhaps through a monthly installment plan, to provide a "hedge against inflation." The New York Stock Exchange has estimated that, through these institutions, more than 100 million Americans today share indirectly in the benefits of equity investment. A classic illustration of this was given by General Wood, then chairman of the board of trustees of the Sears, Roebuck & Company Savings and Profit Sharing Plan, in a statement before the Senate Committee on Banking and Currency:

This lady was a little Polish girl that started to work [at Sears] in the old days, at 15 years of age. She got $6 a week. She now takes care of the financial files of the company and gets, I think, about $80 a week. She put in $4,800 over a period of 37 years [in the Sears Pension Fund]. She took out $4,500 to buy a little house for herself and her parents, so she has invested in the fund now, a net of $275. She has 1,380 shares in the fund, which are worth $104,000 and she has $17,000 in cash. That is a total of $121,000. I do not believe anywhere in the world, except in the United States, and anywhere except at Sears, a working girl would accumulate $121,000 in capital. And she is not alone. There are plenty of others like her.

In fact, every employee who has been with us for over 30 years gets out, no matter how humble their position, with a minimum capital of $50,000 which may go up to $150,000. In other words, we are making capitalists every year.[1]

As a matter of convenience, institutional investors are sometimes classified as savings and nonsavings types, although it does not appear that such classification greatly facilitates analysis of their development or their functions in the economy. Savings institutions are generally considered as including life insurance companies, savings banks, savings and loan associations, pension funds and investment companies. The nonsavings institutions are generally thought to include fire and casualty insurance companies, foundations, and institutional endowments of colleges, universities, and hospitals.

Commercial banks do not fit neatly into either of these categories, although, with $98 billion in time and savings deposits, they are clearly a substantial savings institution, exceeded in size only by life insurance companies. And while it is true that most banks act as financial *intermediaries*, the broad discretion normally granted to them in instruments of trust makes them comparable to other institutions.

The growth of institutional investors in recent years has been dramatic. Total assets of savings institutions, exclusive of commercial banks, have increased from $37 billion in 1929 to $361.7 billion

[1] *Senate Committee on Banking and Currency, Hearings on Factors Affecting the Buying and Selling of Equity Securities,* 84th Cong., 1st Sess., at 505 (1955).

in 1962. During this same period, the Gross National Product rose 431 per cent, from $104.4 billion annually to $554.8 billion. Savings institutions have grown more than twice as fast as the economy as a whole. At the same time nonsavings institutions have accelerated 694 per cent from $7.06 billion in 1929 to $56.07 billion in 1962.

The most striking growth rates have been those of mutual funds and pension funds. After alternate spasms of rapid growth and stagnation in the 1930's, mutual funds ascended from $500 million in 1936 to $4 billion in 1952. And from 1953 to 1958 the asset value of mutual funds tripled from $4 billion to $12 billion. Over thirty-three years, from 1929 to 1962, mutual fund assets have grown from $134 million to over $22.9 billion, an increase of over 17,000 per cent. This represented an industry come of age. No longer could things be as they were in 1924 when Massachusetts Investors Trust, the first American mutual fund, extended to its shareholders the right to redeem their shares.

Economic growth also came rapidly for the noninsured corporate pension funds. From 1929 to 1962 their value soared 7,000 per cent, from $500 million to nearly $36 billion. Since the Second World War the combined assets of these two institutions, mutual funds and noninsured corporate pension funds, have increased from $3.98 billion to $58.9 billion, an increase of nearly 1,500 per cent. In the same period total assets of all savings institutions rose 388 per cent, and the Gross National Product, 160 per cent.

The factors that have produced the rapid growth of institutional investors are complex. In 1929 banks and life insurance companies were the firmly established financial leaders. Linked to the economy, they shared in the nation's later prosperity. And, in addition, as personal earnings mounted and became more evenly distributed among the middle- and lower-income groups, hitherto untapped funds became available for investment and saving. Increased personal wealth, together with the continuous and vigorous promotion efforts of the life insurance industry, have made us an insurance-minded nation. So, too, rising personal incomes have been used to acquire more products, which in turn has accelerated the need for fire and casualty insurance. The increasing use of installment buying has had a similar effect, since the suppliers of purchase-money credit customarily require such insurance covering items acquired subject to a chattel mortgage or conditional sale agreement.

Changes in the population make-up, in all likelihood, cause changes in patterns of saving and investing. Urbanization and rising numbers of salaried individuals result in reduced direct investment by individuals and more saving and investing through institutions.

Mutual funds and pension funds were relatively insignificant in 1929. But mutual fund companies have followed the pattern of the life insurance industry, employing vigorous promotion efforts to obtain continuous sales of their shares. Hence, even in periods of declining markets when mutual funds would be expected to be less popular, sales of mutual fund shares have consistently exceeded redemptions. In part this success springs from a prevailing fear of inflation, for mutual funds are primary purchasers of equities and have appealed to the public as the best "hedge against inflation." Of course, their concentration in common stocks has contributed to their rapid growth, as they, more than any other institutions, have reaped the benefits of the great market rise since the end of the Second World War. Nevertheless, sale of additional shares has been the principal source of mutual fund expansion.

The rise of pension funds stems from two factors, aside from the general economic prosperity since the Second World War. First, and perhaps most important, was the decision in *Inland Steel Corp. v. National Labor Relations Board*,[2] which held that an employer has an affirmative duty to bargain with employee representatives on the question of pensions, for this affects both a worker's wages and his conditions of employment as defined under the National Labor Relations Act. From this decision arose new union demands. Pensions became as important an item in collective bargaining as wages. The reasons are obvious: (1) The effect of automation heightens the need for early retirement, which thus becomes a kind of substitute for job security. (2) Taxes begin to sap higher wages, thereby forcing the union to take its increased share of company profits through such fringe benefits as pensions. Certainly these points were established in the automotive negotiations of 1964. The Ford contract, as does the Chrysler pact, calls for a boost in the basic pension rate to $4.25 a month, for every year of service, up from $2.80, and an early retirement provision which will give some workers a company pension of as much as $400 a month at age sixty after thirty years of service.

[2] 170 F. 2d 247 (7th Cir. 1948).

Indeed, the automotive talks emphasized still another phase of benefits that surely will become more important with the passing years: a stock purchase plan for employees. For the first time Chrysler, following precedent already established by Ford and General Motors, offered such a plan to salaried white-collar workers represented by the union.

Further, the provisions of the Internal Revenue Code of 1954 have, in effect, made government a partner with industry in the funding of employee pensions, for pension contributions under a "qualified plan" are tax deductible to the employer. Thus, at the 52 per cent rate, actual cost to the employer is forty-eight cents for each dollar of funded benefit, not counting actuarial accumulation. The Code also provides that such contributions are not taxable income to the employee until he becomes eligible to receive benefits under the plan, and then only at the more favorable capital gains rates.

Charitable foundations and institutional endowments have also benefited from the tax laws. High tax rates in the upper income brackets and the deductibility of charitable contributions have combined to encourage the flow of funds to tax-exempt institutions. Total assets of such institutions increased from $2.4 billion in 1929 to over $21.8 billion in 1962, an increase of over 900 per cent.

THE EXPERTISE OF INSTITUTIONAL INVESTORS

Institutional investors act as intermediaries. They receive funds from the public in the form of bank deposits, trust funds, insurance premiums, and pension fund contributions, and in turn invest them to achieve a given end. While institutional investment objectives may vary substantially, there is one common denominator. The institutions are experts; they are professional investors. Their investment activities are conducted by organizations of men highly trained in the ways of finance. They are staffed with accountants, analysts, and economists who concentrate their studies on a single industry or perhaps even a segment of one.

The measure of an institution's expertise may depend on its size. The more funds there are to invest, the more manpower is necessary to investigate qualified investment opportunities. Presumably, therefore, competence and ability may go with size and specialization.

Yet bigness is not always the salient consideration, for power may come from the manner in which an institution invests its funds. Mutual funds, with assets only one-sixth those of life insurance companies, hold three times as much common stock. What a mutual fund does with any one stock may be expected to have a greater impact upon management of the portfolio corporation than the behavior of an insurance company. Practically, this power might well result in profits to the mutual fund, for the portfolio corporation may be more willing to dispense confidential information, not available to other shareholders, to induce action, either in buying or selling, on the part of the fund. The result, in any event, is power disproportionate to size.

Mutual funds are generally managed under contract by an investment advisor. In theory, though not in fact, the advisor is a separate entity. Typically, the advisory service is owned and controlled by those who founded or control the fund. The investment advisor usually has a professional staff specializing in particular industries who, in addition to reading the published information, spend considerable time in the field where they seek from corporate management that which goes beyond the printed word, in the hope of gaining insights that are not generally available to the public.

Despite the self-proclaimed expertise of the mutual funds, their performance as a whole has been something less than spectacular. The Wharton Report found that, for the five and three-quarters years covered by the study, the Standard and Poors Composite Common Stock Index was definitely superior to the average performance of mutual funds. When adjustments were made for the variations in portfolio structure, that is, for those funds concentrating in particular classes of securities, it was found that the funds' performance "did not differ appreciably from what would have been achieved by an unmanaged portfolio with the same division among asset types. About half the funds performed better, half worse." Only 25 per cent of the common stock funds performed better than the Standard and Poors Index.

Functionally, the organization of banks is not unlike that of the mutual funds, except that their investment advice does not come from a separate legal entity. Trust departments and investment committees within the bank organization are their investment advisors. However, in the case of the very large banks, the size and depth of their organization may be considerably greater than is normally found in even the large mutual funds.

Like the mutual fund, so great is a bank's potentiality for investment that any reasonable question relating to a possible investment is usually answered by corporate management. Often a single pension fund account will equal the total assets of a sizable mutual fund:

> The great growth in number of accounts and the assets handled by trust departments over the past few decades has been accompanied by a radical change in the investment of trusteed funds. During this period an ever-increasing percentage of stocks has been considered prudent. This trend promoted the growth of the investment analysis or statistical section of the trust department. It also witnessed the change in many banks, from a policy largely dominated or influenced by committees of outside directors with no particular qualifications for such work, to a program dictated by skilled advisers and approved by various committees composed of investment and trust officers as well as members of the board of directors.[3]

A bank's influence rests on two grounds, which the law and a bank might try to separate in theory but cannot entirely do in reality. From the trust department come the funds for equity investments, and from the commercial loan department comes credit. Both may be extended to the same corporation by the same bank. In what is disclosed by the corporation to the bank, one might question whether the power aggregate can be ignored.

Inside information, the hint of things to come, becomes a valued commodity to the institutions under constant pressure to make productive use of the monies entrusted to them. It is data affirmatively sought; its successful harvesting can alter institutional investment decisions. Its very nature, however, prevents disclosure to other shareholders. The ability to obtain such confidences is a characteristic in which many institutions take pride; it demonstrates their ability to perform. The basic unfairness to the rest of the investing public is manifest when institutions exercise their power to

[3] Morse, *Committee Organization in Medium Sized Trust Departments,* 98 TRUSTS AND ESTATES 785 (1959).

obtain what is essentially inside information and use that information to change their investment position. While there has been some recognition of this problem, the prevailing view among institutional managements seems to be that they are perfectly free to use whatever information they obtain, from whatever source, as they see fit. The issue became a matter of concern to the Senate Committee investigating the stock market in 1955. An officer of an institutional investor was asked:

> Mr. Wallace: But if you were to buy stock on the open market on the basis of information that you had gotten in conferring with management, would this be considered trading on inside information?
>
> Mr. Graham [Chairman of the Board of the Graham-Newman Corporation of New York]: No sir; because, as I understand the interpretation of the rules, trading on inside information applies only to those who have a fiduciary relationship toward the stockholders, namely, officers, directors, and major stockholders.[4]

Of course, an officer, director, or controlling stockholder clearly cannot trade on inside information without risking liability for fraud under section 17 of the Securities Act and rule 10b-5 under the Securities Exchange Act. And, if he effects "short swing" transactions, as we have noted, his profits from such trading may be recovered by any stockholder under section 16(b). But should there be liability if a corporate officer tells a powerful investor of an anticipated merger, or of a change in the dividend, or of an anticipated stock split? Mr. Graham answered in his testimony before the Senate Committee: "Well, if a feasible method of tightening the law could be devised which would get that objective without countervailing disadvantages of many sorts, I would be for it."

The SEC has demonstrated, however, that the law may not be quite as permissive as Mr. Graham believed. In the *Matter of Cady Roberts & Co.*,[5] a member of a brokerage firm attended a morning meeting of the board of directors of the Curtis Wright Corporation. During a recess in the board's meeting he telephoned his office to pass along the news that the board, of which he was a

[4] *Supra* note 1, at 536.
[5] Sec. Exch. Act Rel. No. 6668 (1961).

member, had cut the forthcoming dividend on the company's common stock. The brokerage firm acted on this information to reduce its own position in Curtis Wright stock and, in addition, sold the stock for certain of its discretionary accounts. Through an apparently inadvertent delay, word of the dividend reduction did not appear on the wire services until the afternoon of the same day, a fact of which the selling broker claimed to be unaware.

The Commission held that the firm had violated the antifraud provisions of section 17(a) of the Securities Act and of rule 10b-5 under the Securities Exchange Act. Despite the firm's assertions that its action was wholly consistent with its fiduciary responsibilities, the wrong was specifically held to apply to the sales effected on behalf of the discretionary accounts. The firm, through its member-director, was deemed an "insider" who had effected sales of securities in interstate commerce without disclosing a material fact that it reasonably should have known was not yet available to the general public.

The implications of this case for institutional investors who obtain and act on information before it becomes public knowledge are apparent. True, the Commission's decision was based on the fact that the firm's representative was a director of the corporation. But just how essential is this formality to the logic of the case? Suppose the firm's representative had simply been invited to attend the directors' meeting, but was not actually a member of the board? Would he have then had the same fiduciary responsibilities? In any event, would his use of corporate information for personal gain have amounted to fraud? It seems probable that the Commission would have little difficulty in reaching that conclusion.

It is common knowledge that, with minor variations, *Cady Roberts* is an everyday occurrence. It is the established pattern for there to be substantial price moves immediately preceding the public announcement of corporate developments. Often these developments are of such proportions that even the nonexpert, if he had known of them, could very well have predicted the market reaction. Indeed, the absence of a significant price move under such circumstances, yet prior to any public release of the significant information, is unusual. Of course, there is public speculation, too—on the basis of rumors. But the consistency with which the pattern is followed leads almost inescapably to the conclusion that often there are some acting on the basis not of rumors but *facts* not generally available to the public. When those who *know* are buyers, there are others who sell in ignorance. Identifying those who consistently seem to be "in the know" could itself be the subject of a work. Is it the institutions? While the evidence is far from conclusive, they are natural suspects.

If significant corporate news becomes known to a broker, he will, of course, be inclined to use it to the extent that a portfolio change might result. Indeed, the ability to predict accurately is the quality that brings him business, not the neatness with which he effects transactions for his principal, nor the fact that he charges lower commissions than his competitors, for this he is not permitted to do. What brings him business is, in sum, his reliability as a source of information concerning when and how the price of stocks will move. Hence, he makes it his business to "scoop" every possible corporate development. When he is successful, to which of his many clients will he tell the choice news? He cannot get in touch with all of them simultaneously, and even if he could, the news would immediately lose its value. Time is of the essence, and it seems unlikely that widows and orphans would stand high on the list of those to be let in on the secret.

If a brokerage firm has institutional clients, their business will likely be much more important than that of any individual. Moreover, institutions frequently are affiliated with brokerage concerns and are thus assured of access to any corporate news the firm obtains. The Wharton Report found the allocation of brokerage to be an "asset" of mutual funds frequently used to obtain investment advice from broker-dealers. And what is true for mutual funds may well be applicable to other institutions as well.

No doubt the large institutions do possess a great deal of investment acumen, but their probable access to inside information and their consistent concentration in the safer "blue chip" stocks (discussed more fully in the next chapter) tend to tarnish somewhat the image of financial wizardry.

While the prevailing view may be that existing securities laws strike only at the "insider" who abuses his position of trust, the wolf is certainly at the door for the institutions in the *Cady Roberts* case. For one thing, the definition of "insider" for purposes of rule 10b-5 is by no means clear. Moreover, the rule applies by its terms to *any person* who, in the purchase or sale of a security, makes any misrepresentation of a material fact or fails to declare that necessary to make the facts stated not misleading or who engages in any device, artifice, or scheme to defraud. While the unaffiliated "tippee" may now be free to act on the basis of his tips, the day may come when the Commission and the courts will think otherwise.

With insurance companies, however, the development of investment expertise has been a function of their concentration in private purchases of senior securities, as opposed to the purchase of common stocks in the open market. Since the adoption of the Securities Act of 1933, public offerings of corporate securities have declined steadily in relation to private placements—the sale of securities to a limited number of offerees, usually institutions, who acquire them for investment. From 1934 to 1963, $65.1 billion of corporate securities were sold privately while $127.3 billion were offered publicly. In 1962, a big year for public offerings, $6.1 billion of securities were sold to the public, while $4.6 billion were offered privately. In the first six months of 1963, the ratio of public to private offerings was $3.08 billion to $3.25 billion. The reasons for this development are in part related to the passage of the Securities Act of 1933. The costs of flotation of a public issue have been substantially increased by the registration and prospectus provisions.

Indeed, expenses of $100,000 or more may be incurred in marketing a large public issue. Added to this are underwriting fees, discounts, and commissions of from 4.5 per cent to 9.5 per cent of the aggregate public offering price. If debt securities are sold publicly, additional expenses are incurred by the appointment of a trustee and compliance with the Trust Indenture Act of 1939. Private placements, on the other hand, are exempt from the act's requirements and are thus less costly for the issuing company. To a lesser degree, the switch to private placements may have been a management attempt to avoid statutory personal liabilities of those who sign the registration statement. Convenience no doubt is a factor, too. The enormous effort of gathering and shaping the information required in a prospectus necessarily disrupts company routine.

Probably more important, however, has been the availability of life insurance funds resulting from their rapid growth and the reluctance of corporate managements to dilute the outstanding equity when adequate capital could be obtained either by borrowing at favorable rates or out of retained earnings. In addition, the deductibility of interest for tax purposes has encouraged the issuance of debt securities, which are more salable to insurance companies than to a public eager for equity growth and capital gains.

The insurance industry welcomed the opportunity to supply new capital; it provided a lawful investment source for the mounting deposits of policy-holders. Indeed, it was only recently that insurance companies were permitted to purchase common stocks. Even now limitations are imposed on the percentage of assets devoted to common or preferred issues, and corporate debt obligations.

Corporate borrowing at one time was largely limited to obligations secured by fixed assets. Experience demonstrated, however, that they were not necessarily safer than other securities. Thus, borrowing on retained and future earnings became more prevalent. Still, to make such loans safely, the lender must have intimate knowledge of the borrower's overall soundness. It is in this respect that the investment expertise of life insurance companies comes to the fore. Investment analysts inspect the prospective borrower's physical plants, review corporate books, and check inventory methods and adequacy of internal controls. Extensive discussions are held with management officials, company auditors, and counsel; certified financial statements are normally required for at least the last five years. Projections of income for the pay-out period are prepared by the management under the supervision of the company's auditors, although, of course, no auditors' certificates can be given with respect to such projections, other than the accountants' informal assurance that they appear to be reasonable on the basis of the company's prior history.

Loan and note agreements developed by the large insurance companies and their counsel are veritable masterpieces of legal draftsmanship. Strict provisions are often included limiting the company's right to pay dividends, incur additional indebtedness, encumber or dispose of its property, acquire additional assets, make capital investments or long-term lease obligations in excess of specified limits, issue or acquire additional securities, or merge or consolidate with other companies. The agreements of each company appear to be uniform in many respects, but they are actually tailored, on the basis of extensive negotiations, to meet the individual needs of the borrower while maintaining maximum security for the insurance company's investment. Elaborate and complicated provisions are inserted to effect subordination of all other indebtedness, and the default provisions customarily give the insurance company the right to accelerate the due date. And, to illustrate the eagerness of the insurance companies to maintain their investments, premiums are imposed if the indebtedness is prepaid, at least if it is prepaid from other outside financing, and the borrower is usually required to give the lending insurance company the first right to furnish any additional financing that the borrower may need during the pay-out period.

The insurance companies have shown flexibility in their approach to private placements and thus acquired diverse portfolios of notes, bonds, debentures, and preferred stocks which are sometimes convertible into common stock at the option of the holder. One very good measure of their investment expertise is the minimal amount of their realized losses on portfolio securities purchased privately. Indeed, the average mutual fund holder might well wish his fund had a similar record with respect to its purchases of common stocks.

INVESTMENT POLICIES AND PORTFOLIO MAKE-UP

The shaping of institutional investment policy is affected by many factors: the nature of the institution, the role it plays in the financial community, the types of services it provides, the necessity for liquidity. With life insurance companies and banks, for example, there are added federal and state legal restrictions, principally designed to insure solvency, with the resulting emphasis on extremely conservative investments. Tax considerations may also be important. Regulated investment companies can avoid all federal income tax by passing on at least 90 per cent of income to their stockholders, but again, limitations are imposed on portfolio make-up as a condition of the favored tax treatment.

Thus, as might be expected, investment policies vary among different types of institutions. Mutual funds and pension funds are heavily concentrated in equity securities. Savings and loan associations and mutual savings banks own little or no equity securities, while foundations and institutional endowments seem to strike a closer balance between common stocks and fixed-income obligations. Even among those that invest in common stocks there are significant differences in investment policies. Pension funds and insurance companies invest in more conservative securities with a lower turnover rate while mutual funds tend to buy so-called growth stocks, looking to capital gains, and have a somewhat higher turnover rate.

Yet the overriding characteristic of all institutional investment is conservatism. "Blue Chip" stocks, or the "favorite fifty," are overwhelming institutional favorites. New ventures and unseasoned securities are avoided. Needless to say, the prevalence of this policy has had a serious effect on the availability of capital for fledgling enterprises and small businesses. In fact, it was the shortage of capital for new enterprises that in part prompted passage of the Investment Company Act of 1940 and, more recently, the Small Business Investment Act of 1958.

Noninsured Pension Funds. The year 1962 found private (nongovernment) pension funds with assets of $60.7 billion, of which approximately $36 billion were noninsured corporate pension plans, about $3 billion union noninsured private plans, and approximately $21.6 billion insured plans. The $36 billion of noninsured corporate pension funds had a market value at December 31, 1962, of $40.3 billion. About 75 per cent of all private noninsured plans were in the form of trusts, administered primarily by banks.

Pension plans are established to provide retirement benefits for beneficiaries or their survivors. Normally contributions are actuarially computed to result in fixed payments from a given date. The formula is based upon assumed rates of retirement and income to the fund from interest and dividends. Since earned income in excess of the assumed figures can result in reduced future contributions by the employer, pension funds are generally invested in a combination of common stocks and high-grade corporate bonds, looking to the highest yield consistent with reasonable safety. At year-end 1962 common stock investments of corporate pension funds amounted to $15.7 billion or 39 per cent of fund assets, while corporate bond investment amounted to $16.7 billion, or 45 per cent of fund assets. Holdings in government securities, once popular with pension accounts, have thus been reduced from 31 per cent of fund assets in 1951 to a mere 6 per cent in 1962. While the dollar amounts of government obligations have remained relatively stable over the past ten years, fund investments in corporate bonds and common stocks have increased sharply, with equities dramatically rising from 11 per cent in 1951 to 39 per cent in 1962. Corporate pension plans now hold more common stock than any other single class of institutions. At the end of 1963 the market value of their holdings of common stocks was more than $25 billion.

More recently, the advent of variable benefit plans has accelerated the institutional move to common stocks. In such plans the sum paid at retirement will depend on the investment experience of a segregated portion of the total fund, which would likely be invested entirely in equities, with emphasis on growth stocks. As variables become more popular, pension fund investments in common stocks will doubtless be further emphasized.

From the standpoint of effective investment, trusteed pension plans occupy an enviable position. Since they are tax exempt, they are not inhibited by the prospects of realizing capital gains. Their obligations are largely fixed and predictable so that liquidity is not a problem. In addition, the legal restrictions on trustees' investments, though relatively liberal, are usually waived in the trust instrument, giving the trustee the widest possible discretion. However, in some cases limitations are imposed to avoid entanglement with the employer company, in part because of potential tax questions. Like most other institutions, pension plans do not seek to gain control, but rather to insure diversification. A notable exception is the Sears plan, which concentrates in Sears stock and now holds nearly 30 per cent of the company's outstanding shares.

Pension plans buy for the long haul. Their estimated portfolio turnover rate is well below the NYSE average. They have been net purchasers of common and preferred stocks in every year since 1957 by at least $1 billion annually, and since 1961 they have been net purchasers by over $2 billion per year. In 1962 pension fund net purchases of common stock were equivalent to 80 per cent of net new equity issues during the year.

Investment Companies. Investment companies are of two principal types—open-end management companies ("mutual funds") and closed-end management companies. Unit investment trusts and face amount certificate companies, also specifically mentioned in the Investment Company Act of 1940, are no longer significant. The basic difference between mutual funds and closed-end companies is the factor of redeemability of shares. Mutual funds stand ready to redeem their shares at all times at their then net asset value, in some cases less a small redemption premium. At the same time, most mutual funds are continuously offering new shares to the public. A number of closed-end companies are listed on the major securities exchanges, but mutual funds cannot be listed, for there is very little trading in their shares. At the end of 1962, total assets of all investment companies were $29.4 billion, of which $22.9 billion were held by mutual funds and $6.5 billion by closed-end companies. Since nearly half of all closed-end company assets were held by a single nondiversified company, this discussion will relate primarily to mutual funds. It can be said in passing, however, that the policy of concentration in common stocks is followed by both types of investment companies. In 1962 mutual funds held $17.6 billion in common stocks, representing 82.7 per cent of their total assets. Holdings of New York Stock Exchange listed stocks by mutual funds and closed-end companies at the end of 1963 were estimated at $19 billion and $5.7 billion, respectively, slightly less than the amount of such holdings by pension funds, the largest single type of institution in terms of total listed stock holdings.

Fund objectives primarily determine the flow of their monies. For example, most funds function as either balanced funds, common stock funds, specialty funds or single industry group funds, or preferred stock or bond funds.

The Investment Company Act of 1940 requires that investment companies be registered with the Securities and Exchange Commission. The registration statement and any prospectus used in offering the company's shares to the public must contain a full disclosure of the fund's investment policy, which must include a commitment to either a diversified or nondiversified investment portfolio. If the option is to diversify, the company is required to maintain at least 75 per cent of its assets in cash items, government obligations, the securities of other investment companies, or securities limited in respect of any one issuer to no more than 5 per cent of the total assets of the investment company and to no more than 10 per cent of the outstanding voting securities of such issuer. The investment policies of an investment company cannot be changed in the absence of shareholder approval.

More is known about mutual funds than other institutions as a result of the Wharton Report, *A Study of Mutual Funds,* prepared for the Securities and Exchange Commission by the Wharton

School of Finance and Commerce. Some of its findings with respect to the investment policies of mutual funds are summarized below. The report relates primarily to the period from December 1952 to September 1958.

At September 30, 1958, the funds as a group had 93.5 per cent of their assets invested in corporate securities. The smaller funds tended to invest defensively by retaining greater liquidity. Liquidity appeared to be more or less inversely related to size, which presumably is based on the diminishing likelihood of a proportionately large demand for redemptions, as funds increase in size. However, the principal differences in portfolio make-up resulted from diverse investment objectives. At the close of the study period, common stock funds were 87 per cent invested in common stocks, down from a high of 91 per cent in 1952; bonds and preferred stocks represented 3 per cent and 2 per cent of their total assets, respectively. Balanced funds were 63 per cent invested in common stocks, 15 per cent in preferred stocks, and 14 per cent in bonds.

Rates of portfolio turnover varied greatly, from a high of over 200 per cent in one year for one broker-affiliated fund (assets: $27.7 million) to less than 10 per cent for some of the larger funds. As might be expected, there was a consistent inverse correlation between size and rate of portfolio turnover, expressed as a percentage of total assets (adjusted for net money inflow and outflow in each year). During the period studied the turnover rates for the industry increased from 17.6 per cent to 23.6 per cent. The *equity* turnover rate for the industry exceeded that of the New York Stock Exchange for all listed stocks and in 1958 rose to 16.9 per cent for the industry as compared to 12.9 per cent on the Exchange. Yet there were exceptions. In one year 15 per cent of all funds had turnover rates of less than 10 per cent. Based on a special one-week study conducted by the New York Stock Exchange, turnover rates for mutual funds were recently estimated at 20.1 per cent, substantially higher than any other institution, of which the next highest was 14.8 per cent for noninsured corporate pension funds. These figures can be compared with the estimated average of 21.0 per cent for all shares listed on the Exchange, which necessarily includes the activities of specialists, odd-lot dealers, and floor traders, whose turnover rates are understandably high.

Mutual funds were substantial net purchasers throughout the

period studied. Their net purchases of all securities rose from $365.3 million in 1953 to over $1 billion for the first nine months of 1958. Net purchases of common and preferred stocks rose from $326 million in 1953 to $756 million in the first nine months of 1958.

Insurance Companies. Insurance companies are of two primary categories: life insurance and fire and casualty companies. In terms of size the life companies are by far the most important. In 1962 more than $700 billion of life insurance was in effect in the United States, and life insurance companies held assets of $133.2 billion. At the same time fire and casualty companies' assets totaled approximately $34 billion. The nature and functions of life companies are substantially different from those of fire and casualty, and these differences are reflected in their investment policies. While both are extensively regulated by state laws designed to insure solvency and protect policyholders, and both are required to maintain substantial reserves, the cash flow requirements of life companies are relatively stable and predictable, permitting a low degree of liquidity, whereas the fire and casualty companies must maintain a high degree of liquidity to cover the risks of major disasters. The fire and casualty companies thus have a larger proportion of their assets invested in municipal and government securities and common stocks. The life companies, relatively speaking, are more heavily invested in corporate bonds and mortgages.

At the end of 1962 life insurance companies had $51.5 billion invested in corporate bonds, representing 38.7 per cent of their total assets and 46 per cent of the aggregate amount of all corporate bonds outstanding in the United States. They are thus by far the largest holders of corporate bonds. At the same time life companies had $46.9 billion invested in mortgages, representing 35.2 per cent of their total assets, and only $4.1 billion or 3.1 per cent of their total assets invested in common stocks. Fire and casualty companies, on the other hand, had over $15.8 billion invested in municipal and government securities, representing 46.4 per cent of their assets while life companies had $11.5 billion or only 8.6 per cent of their total assets invested in these securities. The fire and casualty companies held $10.4 billion of common stocks, representing 30.4 per cent of their total assets.

Legal restrictions on investments in common stock by fire and casualty companies are liberal, while life companies have been much more strictly regulated. Indeed, until recently life companies were not permitted to invest in common stocks at all. In New York, where companies holding 85 per cent of the assets of all life insurance companies are licensed to do business, investments in common stocks are permitted under the following conditions:

(1) Total common stock holdings cannot exceed 5 per cent of the insurance company's total assets or 50 per cent of its capital and surplus, whichever is less.

(2) Investment in a single issue may not exceed 2 per cent of such issue or 2 per cent of the insurance company's assets, whichever is less.

(3) To be eligible for purchase by life insurance companies, a common stock issue must (a) have paid dividends for at least the past ten years, (b) have had earnings at least sufficient to cover dividend payments in each of such years, and (c) (except for the stock of banks and insurance companies) be listed on a national securities exchange.

(4) In addition, there is a so-called basket provision which permits insurance companies to invest up to 2 per cent of their total assets in securities that do not meet the requirements of the statute, but the purchase of common stocks under this provision is limited to 50 per cent of capital and surplus.

There are also restrictions on the purchase of debt securities and preferred stocks by life insurance companies. In general, up to 20 per cent of a preferred stock issue may be purchased, provided it does not exceed 2 per cent of the insurance company's assets. Debt securities are eligible for purchase by life companies if the issuer's earnings have been at least equal to one and one-half times "fixed charges," as defined in the statute, for the past five years and for at least two of the past three years. The life insurance companies have thus been forced to concentrate in senior securities and even their limited investments in common stocks have been confined to "blue chips." What is more, the securities they buy are retained; their portfolio turnover rates are estimated to be among the lowest of all institutions.

The legal restrictions imposed on life investments, coupled with the need for stable income to meet the fixed dollar obligations, have stimulated life companies' concentration in the private purchase of corporate securities. Expertise in this area has enabled the life companies to seek out and investigate high quality securities and obtain the protections necessary to insure stability of income. As we have noted, the life companies have thus become the leaders in private placement financing.

But another result of these strict investment limitations can be seen in the trend of pension funds toward trusteed, rather than insured, plans. The effects of this were aptly described by the president of The Equitable Life Assurance Society of the United States in a statement before the Joint Legislative Committee on Insurance Rates and Regulation of the State of New York:

> In 1950 insured and trusteed plans shared the field on roughly a 50–50 basis in terms of total funds held for advance funding. At the end of 1957, the ratio stood at about 60–40 in favor of trusteed plans. Today the spread is even greater, and a large majority of the new large plans and many smaller ones are being established on the trusteed basis. Expanding economy produces a natural growth in pension plans, but the important point is that trusteed plans show a much greater rate of growth than insured plans and the position of the insurance companies has deteriorated substantially relative to trusteed plans. In 1950, contributions to trusteed plans were only 22% greater than contributions to insured plans. In 1957, pension trust contributions were 87% greater than those to insured plans.[6]

Investments under trusteed plans are generally limited only by the provisions of the trust agreement, and substantial portions of such funds may be invested in equities. In an expanding and inflationary economy, this has resulted in an increasing income and the capital enhancement of many such funds, permitting the employer to enlarge benefits or decrease contributions to the fund. Under insured plans comparable benefits cannot be expected, since payments toward purchase of annuities must be invested by insurance companies within the rigid limitations imposed on them by law.

[6] Statement of James F. Oates, Jr., on January 23, 1959, before The Joint Legislative Committee on Insurance Rates and Regulation of the State of New York.

Foundations and Institutional Endowments. The investment policies of foundations and institutional endowments are difficult to classify. Generally, they tend to be conservative, but substantial portions are in common stocks, simply because they are frequent recipients of such donations. Individuals who have a low tax basis in stock holdings that have greatly increased in value can avoid a large capital gains tax and, at the same time, reduce the size of their taxable estate by making gifts of stock to tax-exempt institutions. So it is that foundation portfolios often are weighted in a single issue. About half of college and university endowments and two-thirds of private foundations are in common stock.

Generally, there are no limitations on the investment policies of these institutions, other than the charter or other governing instrument. As a rule they invest for yield and growth, in safe securities that produce current income to finance operations without invading principal. Liquidity, therefore, is not a problem. Since these institutions are tax exempt, tax considerations do not play a part in shaping investment policies.

Other Institutions. At the end of 1962 some thirty-five hundred trust companies and trust departments of commercial banks held assets of personal trust funds in the amount of $62 billion, of which two thirds, or roughly $40 billion, was in common stocks. This is over twice the amount of common stocks held by either mutual funds or pension funds. While these funds are in a sense individual share owners, they are usually administered by banks and trust companies, under agreements frequently giving the trustee-bank virtually unlimited investment discretion. They thus form a vital part of the institutional picture. A special study of bank intermediary volume of trading on the New York Stock Exchange found that trading on behalf of personal trusts was exceeded only by that effected for pension funds. Trading on behalf of trusts and estates accounted for 24 per cent of all bank and trust company volume during the period studied.

Common trust funds are another form of institution that invests in common stocks. They represent a consolidation of personal trust funds that are too small for efficient administration on an individual basis. The personal trust accounts that make up such a fund are usually less than $100,000. At the end of 1963 common trust funds held assets of $3.6 billion, of which $1.7 billion, or approximately 49 per cent, was in common stocks. While not important in itself, this represents an addition to the total of bank intermediary holdings.

Other institutional investors, such as mutual savings banks, savings and loan associations, and state and local pension funds, are important in size but are not major purchasers of common stocks. Savings and loan associations, for example, have assets estimated at well over $100 billion, but generally they do not invest in corporate securities. Common and preferred stockholdings of mutual savings banks and state and local pension funds amounted to less than $1.7 billion in 1962.

3

〔〔〔〔〔〔〔〔

INSTITUTIONAL
CONCENTRATES AND
MARKET IMPACT

The fiduciary nature of institutions accounts in large part both for their impact on the market and, more precisely, their preference for selected stocks, the "favorite fifty" on the New York Stock Exchange. Neither law nor reality is likely to change this one dominant, common characteristic, namely that of being a fiduciary. Banks will continue in their capacities as trustees of pension funds and personal trusts, of which the combined investments in common stocks represent nearly $100 billion. And investment and insurance companies will remain fiduciaries because statutes so dictate.

The result of this is the seeking out of seasoned enterprises with long and consistent records of earnings and dividends, for even the "prudent man rule" has its bounds. Practically, a fiduciary even with the broadest investment discretion generally will not risk his beneficiary's funds as venture capital without express authority. Legally, the trustee that does not have such discretionary authority in the trust instrument is confined by law to the purchase of "legals," the bluest of the "blue chip" issues.

The New York Stock Exchange found in 1964 that 14.5 per cent of institutional holdings of listed securities were in the Exchange's 5 largest listed companies; 41 per cent were in the 51 largest issues; and 70.6 per cent in the 171 largest issues.

Statistics, however, can be misleading. Stated as a percentage of the issues' aggregate market values, institutions hold about 4.5 per cent of the five largest issues traded on the Big Board. If the holdings of trust funds are included, total institutional holdings of the five largest companies may reach 6.7 per cent of their aggregate market value. If this percentage figure seems low, it should be remembered that the total market value of these five issues—AT&T, IBM, Jersey Standard, du Pont, and GM—exceeds $100 billion. In other words, the value of these five issues is over 25 per cent of the market value of *all* stock listed on the New York Stock Exchange. In addition, all of the big five issues are extremely widely held. The broad distribution of Telephone stock, with over *2,600,000* shareholders, undoubtedly depresses the relative aggregate holdings by institutions of these five giants.

Going beyond the five largest issues, the percentage of total institutional holdings increases sharply. Of the forty-one largest issues on the Big Board, each with a market value of over $1 billion, we find that institutions hold about 25.7 per cent. Again, if the holdings of personal trusts are included, the total institutional holdings of the forty-one largest issues may reach 38 to 40 per cent of the combined value of these issues. And the significance of institutional holdings of the Big Board's largest issues is further emphasized by the fact that these forty-one issues alone account for well over half the market value of *all* securities listed on the NYSE. When we consider the significance of institutional holdings in this group, as a percentage of total institutional holdings of NYSE listed securities, we find that nearly *half* of the institutions' listed portfolio is comprised of securities of the Big Board's forty-one largest issues. While specific stocks are not identified, most, if not all, of these issues undoubtedly figure prominently in the institutions' "favorite fifty." Thus, the conclusion is inescapable that the "favorite fifty" are really favorite. The institutions hold nearly 40 per cent of the relatively few stocks that account for over half the value of all NYSE listed securities, and at the same time these holdings account for half the value of all institutional holdings of Big Board stocks. The concentrators concentrate in the concentrated.

This conclusion finds further support from an examination of institutional holdings in the "smaller" issues. There are slightly over five hundred issues on the Big Board, each of which has a total market value of less than $50 million. In other words, this group includes roughly 40 per cent of the total *number* of issues listed on the NYSE. Yet the institutions' commitment in this category is relatively modest; their total holdings in this group amount to only 1.8 per cent of their portfolio of listed securities. Obviously the institutions are not interested in gambling on the future of the Big Board's smaller, and frequently younger, companies. They prefer to concentrate instead in the shares of the country's largest enterprises. There is, of course, another side to this coin. If institutions invested the same percentage of *their* assets in the smaller companies as they have in the Big Board giants, their concentration in individual issues might be much higher. Since the smaller companies have fewer securities outstanding, not only would major institutional holdings in these issues be less liquid, but the legal and practical complications that spring from "control" would be more likely to arise.

Thus, the pattern of institutional concentration seems to run fairly consistently throughout the industry, irrespective of the type of institution. This is not to say that institutions do not differ in their investment policies. Indeed, they do. Foundations and endowments can be expected to hold a disproportionately larger percentage of the smaller issues, as they are frequent recipients of stock of family enterprises. But, interestingly enough, foundations and endowments represent a relatively small percentage of all institutional assets.

And, of course, some types of institutions are much more deeply committed to equities, in general, than others. Mutual funds and noninsured pension funds, for example, each account for approximately 25 per cent of total institutional common stock holdings. In the case of pension funds, approximately three-fourths in asset value are managed by a dozen New York banks. If we make the further assumption that these same banks control a similar percentage of all stocks held by personal and common trust funds, foundations, endowments, and other nonprofit organizations, it appears that a dozen institutions alone control approximately $50 billion of common stock, or over 12 per cent of the aggregate market value of all stocks listed on the NYSE!

Bank concentration in recent years has resulted in large part

from the rather furious rate of merger activity. The success of the
Justice Department in blocking the mergers of banks in Philadelphia
and in Lexington, Kentucky (as discussed in later chapters) is of
great interest from the standpoint of the application of the federal
antitrust laws to the banking industry. Nevertheless, as far as the
mergers of the giant New York City banks are concerned, the
move seems "too little, too late." The past fifteen years have
seen the Chase National merge with the Bank of the Manhattan
Company; J.P. Morgan & Co. with Guaranty Trust Company of
New York; Chemical Corn Exchange Bank (itself the result of a
merger in 1954) with New York Trust Company; and Manufacturers Trust Company with the Hanover Bank. Only the last of
of these has raised an eyebrow at the Justice Department. Whether
the Federal District Court's recent holding that the Manufacturers
Trust-Hanover merger violated the antitrust laws will jeopardize
other New York bank marriages remains to be seen.

The Philadelphia and Lexington cases, over the jealous objections of the Comptroller of the Currency, at last may have provided
the Department with the weapons it needs to deal with further bank
concentration. Until now the only inhibiting factor seems to have
been the inconvenience of merging large institutions, although as a
practical matter, the New York City banks' place among the silent
partners in American business could have an important bearing on
future mergers between the banks.

A major problem in any trust department consolidation is
the limitation of investment choice placed upon the merged
bank as trustee. The dictates of a prudent investment policy
restrict the number of companies in which a trust department
will invest: the "blue chips" become even bluer because of
the buying interest of institutional investors.

At the same time the larger an institutional investor becomes the greater risk it runs that it will assume a controlling
position in individual companies. From its point of view this is
undesirable not only because of its policy not to influence
management; if it takes a controlling position in a company, it
may someday become difficult to sell out without a loss.[1]

[1] Kraus, *Banks' Role as Silent Partners Limits Their Merger Prospects*, N.Y.
Times, Oct. 20, 1959, Sec. 3 (Financial) p. 1, cols. 2, 3, p. 12, cols. 3, 4.

Mutual funds have not been lacking in concentration either. The Wharton study found that of a total of 156 funds in 1958, only three had assets in excess of $600 million. These three funds had combined assets of $3.29 billion, equal to 26.8 per cent of the industry total. Twenty-one companies, each with assets of $150 million or more, controlled 67.5 per cent of industry assets. Three multicompany groups in the $600 million class held over $4.07 billion, or 33.2 per cent, of industry assets at September 30, 1958. By 1961 the four largest open-end companies accounted for held assets of $6.38 billion, or 28.3 per cent of the industry total. Assuming the typical preponderance of common-stock buying in the mutual fund industry, these *four* must control equities having a market value equal to nearly 1.5 per cent of all NYSE listed stocks.

Institutional investors possess enormous investing power. Mutual funds, having grown from $12.3 billion in 1958 to $23 billion in 1962, must attribute this primarily to sales of additional shares, representing a net inflow of cash. Similarly, corporate pension funds, having increased their common stock holdings from $20.9 billion in 1961 to $25.4 billion in 1963, achieved their growth primarily through employer contributions, which in 1963 alone amounted to $3.4 billion. Indeed, gross receipts of pension funds from all sources in 1963 amounted to $5.7 billion.

The monies received must be invested. And, as pointed out earlier, common stocks have become the predominant object of institutional investing. Thus, in 1962 and 1963 corporate pension funds alone were net purchasers by more than $2 billion annually. Individuals, on the other hand, have been consistent net sellers over the past decade. When considered with the mounting number of individual shareholders, the conclusion is inescapable that as institutional holdings concentrate, individual share ownership is becoming ever more widely diffused. This condition can be expected to continue, when we remember that institutions buy to hold; their portfolio turnover rate, with the exception of the mutual funds, is substantially lower than the New York Stock Exchange average. Moreover, the great institutional purchasing power is by no means evenly distributed over the total breadth of the market. On the contrary, it is disproportionately concentrated in the "favorite fifty."

At the same time the supply of common stocks has been steadily declining. Net new issues of common and preferred stocks, which were $4.1 billion in 1958 and $5.3 billion in 1961, declined markedly after the stock market break in May 1962. Net new issues of equity securities amounted to $2.6 billion in 1962 and only $800 million in 1963. Throughout the period institutions have been net purchasers, by substantial margins. In 1962 institutions were buyers, on balance, by $4.3 billion, which declined somewhat in 1963 to leave institutions as net buyers by $3.5 billion. At the same time the relative position of individuals has deteriorated steadily. In 1958 individuals were still net buyers by $1.3 billion, but by 1962 they were net *sellers* by $1.9 billion. By 1963 their position as net sellers had increased to nearly $3 billion.

Finally, the position of institutions cannot be measured simply in terms of their percentage ownership of the aggregate market value of all outstanding NYSE listed stock. When viewed in terms of the *particular issues* in which they are most heavily concentrated, institutional holdings assume a much greater significance. While the amount of stock of a particular issue that is actually available at a given time is difficult to determine, the so-called floating supply might be compared to an iceberg: the bulk of the largest issues is below the surface and not available in the market place. The annual turnover rate for AT&T and Jersey Standard is 3 per cent, and for the five largest issues on the Big Board, 4 per cent. The rate is understandably lower for the largest issues—the institutional favorites—than for the smaller ones. The average for all NYSE listed issues is 15 per cent. When viewed in this context, institutional ownership of over 20 per cent of all NYSE listed stocks and, more to the point, their estimated holdings of nearly 40 per cent in aggregate market value of the fifty largest issues, becomes of major proportions. And there is a cyclical factor here; as institutional holdings mount, the floating supply will be reduced at a proportionately greater rate. For, as we have seen, they tend to buy to hold. Hence, a smaller proportion of their holdings will go to make up the floating supply. Thus, it is not surprising to find the Exchange warning that the market by 1970, when institutions are expected to hold over 30 per cent of all listed securities, will be "vastly different" from what it is today.

This is not to imply that the total amount of listed shares has not increased. Indeed it has. In 1929 there were approximately one billion shares listed on the Big Board. This figure had risen to nearly four billion at the end of 1955 and to over eight billion at the end of 1963. Yet only a fraction of this increase has come from new issues; and AT&T alone is responsible for 60 per cent of the net new issue increase. Most have sprung from stock splits. Thus, since 1950, AT&T has had three splits (once three for one); General Motors, two (once three for one); and Chrysler Corporation, three in two years. IBM has split once two for one, twice three for two, three times five for four, declared stock dividends of 5 per cent on four different occasions and of 2½ per cent a similar number of times. Behind these share enlargements, of course, lies greater earning power that in turn has resulted from retained earnings. In that sense, they are comparable to new financing. But they do not reduce the position of institutions *relative* to that of individual shareholders. To the extent that increases by means of stock splits are reflected in institutional portfolios, the floating supply of the split stock is *not* proportionately increased, since institutions are net buyers while individuals are net sellers. Hence, stock splits, which have been more common among the larger institutional favorites, would, if anything, tend to aggravate the position of institutions, as compared to that of individual investors.

Another important factor that has increased the overall supply of NYSE stocks has been the addition of previously unlisted issues. The ability of many companies to meet the Big Board listing standards by demonstrating sufficient growth has been particularly marked recently. In the first six months of 1964, forty previously unlisted issues (which in some cases had been listed on the American Stock Exchange) were admitted to trading on the Big Board. Fifty-nine common stock issues were admitted in 1963, a three-decade high. But, as might be expected, newly listed issues do not automatically become institutional favorites. It may take years after admission to Big Board trading for an industrial concern to work its way into the "favorite fifty."

Since institutional trading cannot be isolated from other forces in the market, the impact of institutional activity on market conditions cannot be measured with precision. Nevertheless, the consensus is that institutions *have* contributed in substantial measure to the overall upward trend since the Second World War that has carried stock prices to a succession of record highs. Opinions differ only concerning the degree to which institutions have been responsible for the rise. Institutions would tend to minimize their importance, feeling perhaps a bit nervous over the possibility of additional government regulation, or congressional investigation like that conducted of the 1955 stock market. One wonders if the institutions do not protest too loudly, if their denials of stock market influence may not spring from a knowledge—the kind of knowledge no one else has—of just how influential they are. In any event, the Exchange seems to be firmly in their camp, but it, too, may suffer from some of the same kind of self-interest. There is a respectable school of thought that institutional purchasing has been a force of *major significance* in the market since 1945.

The New York Stock Exchange has conducted a series of "spot checks" of selected days' trading since 1955, as well as a two-day study of May 28 and 29, 1962, which marked the last major market recession (not counting the day President Kennedy was assassinated).

The two-day study in May 1962 covered a period of the most violent price swings and the most active trading of any like period since before the Second World War. For that reason it may be of limited value as a clue to understanding the impact of institutional behavior during more "normal" times. Nevertheless, it is interesting to note that on May 28, institutions were net purchasers by 1.2 million shares and on May 29 they were net purchasers by 1.4 million shares. This would seem to indicate that institutions tend to have a stabilizing influence in the market. However, this is not entirely borne out by the Wharton Report, at least insofar as mutual funds are concerned, and therefore may not be typical of institutional conduct in periods of more moderate price fluctuation. While the Wharton study found that the funds' day-to-day and intraday purchases show some tendency to counter the short-term price trend, primarily because of the use of limited orders, they tend to trade with, rather than against, major cyclical price trends.

The Exchange also conducted a study of trading during the week of October 21 to 25, 1963, that focused primarily on institutional behavior. This study found that institutional investors accounted for approximately 25 per cent of total share volume during the week. Among institutions so-called bank intermediary volume has consistently accounted for the largest portion of institutional activity, although it was down from 40 per cent of all institutional volume in 1960 to 34 per cent in 1963. Mutual funds and non-member brokers and dealers accounted for 17.9 per cent and 11.2 per cent of institutional volume, respectively, figures substantially unchanged from the 1960 study. Institutions paid an average of $48 per share compared with an average price of $41 per share paid by all other investors, again reflecting the institutions' preference for higher quality stocks. The most significant change in the make-up of bank volume was a 470 per cent increase in purchases on behalf of pension funds. It was this source that accounted for two-thirds of the growth in total share volume for the banks from 1955 to 1963. While the business of individual clients rose 37 per cent, their share of total bank volume dropped from 20 per cent in 1955 to 12.3 per cent in 1963. Similarly, transactions on behalf of trusts and estates were up 33 per cent from the 1955 study, but their relative share of total bank volume fell from 41 per cent to 24.3 per cent. Both of these relative "reductions" are obviously the results of the tremendous growth of pension funds.

Perhaps the most dramatic figure to come from the 1963 study was that 63 per cent of all bank dealings were on a fiduciary basis. Moreover, in 43.5 per cent of such transactions, the banks were given full investment discretion as contrasted to 27.7 per cent in 1955. Again, this increase is probably due in large part to the rapid growth of pension funds, which have become the most significant factor in bank intermediary trading.

More is known of the market impact of mutual funds, through the efforts of the Wharton study. It concluded that the spiraling increase of funds' net purchases of common stock has "stimulated stock prices markedly over the past decade or so."[2] In addition, continuous selling of mutual fund shares brought monies into the market in amounts substantially greater than would otherwise have been invested in securities.

Like all institutions, the overall market influence of mutual funds was less than that in selected issues. At the peak of fund

[2] The Wharton School of Finance and Commerce, *A Study of Mutual Funds*, Prepared for the Securities and Exchange Commission, H.R. REP. No. 2274, 87th Cong., 2d Sess. 21 (1962).

activity, gross purchases were less than 10 per cent of total NYSE volume and, with rare exceptions, net purchases were less than 5 per cent of NYSE volume. Nevertheless, the report stated:

> There is some but not strong evidence that mutual funds significantly affect the month-to-month movements in the stock market as a whole. There is strong evidence that fund net purchases significantly affect the daily movements in the stock market, and the statistical results suggest that this effect may be fairly substantial.[3]

With respect to thirty issues considered the "mutual fund favorites," the report found:

> These 30 issues on the average rose considerably more in price than the stock market as a whole over the 1953-58 period covered, and there is a significant correlation between the percentage increase in price of each issue and the volume of fund net purchases relative to New York Stock Exchange volume. The funds showed a definite tendency to buy on balance in the 2 months prior to cyclical upswings in the prices of these individual issues and to sell on balance (or to have weaker purchase balances) in the 2 months prior to cyclical downswings, giving some support to the hypothesis that fund activity may have been partially responsible for (and may have partially forecast) the major phenomenon that mutual funds as a whole may to some extent have the ability to fulfill their own market predictions, and in particular to validate their own appraisal of individual issues.[4]

These facts have been related in an effort to show the power position of institutional investors in relation to other shareholders. The facts call forth the following analysis. The behavior of institutional investors is a factor in raising or lowering the level of the stock market. This was, in part, the thrust of the Senate investigation of the "Bull" market in 1955:

> The rise of institutional purchases was frequently mentioned as one of the factors responsible for the stock-market rise.

[3] *Ibid.*
[4] *Id.* at 22.

It was asserted that, as recipients of mounting flows of cash which are increasingly invested in stocks, they influence the demand price for stocks, and as semipermanent investors, they reduce the "floating" supply, particularly of "blue chips."[5]

It is difficult, as the Senate committee concluded, to measure the precise impact of institutional investors on the market. It is fair to state, however, that they have substantial influence and accordingly are in part responsible for causing the rise or fall of the price of stock of other shareholders. They have more influence than any individual, for they hold much larger investments.

This thought leads to another. Institutions are rapidly reaching a point where it may be impracticable and unprofitable for them to sell their holdings of particular issues. The Commissioner of Corporations for the State of California wrote in 1960:

> As the stocks held by these institutions, and by clients of investment advisers, continue to account for larger and larger proportions of all securities, their freedom of action will apparently become limited by their total size. The so-called "Wall Street Rule"—sell the stock if you don't like what the management is doing—may not be feasible in the future for an investor with large holdings in a stock in which the principal holders are also institutional investors. Only a few would be able to sell out in such a market without depressing the price so greatly that it would be uneconomic to sell.[6]

The argument is made that many institutional investors, either by agreement or as a matter of policy, will limit their acquisitions in any given corporation. Thus, General Motors has asked the trustees of its pension plan not to acquire more than 5 per cent of a company's voting stock.[7] Mr. McCloy, then with the Chase National Bank, testified:

---

[5] Senate Committee on Banking and Currency, *Stock Market Study*, S. REP. No. 376, 84th Cong., 1st Sess. 7 (1955).

[6] Sobieski, *In Support of Cumulative Voting*, 15 BUS. LAW. 316, 321 (1960).

[7] Harry S. Benjamin of General Motors Corporation legal staff introduced a long statement of the company's pension fund investment policy to a Senate committee investigating welfare and pension funds. The statement read in part: "Also in order to insure that the trustees and the corporation will avoid any possible charge that control or management responsibility is being acquired in any company through the pension funds, investments of each trustee in the

I must say I am impressed at the moment, at least, by the efforts which are made by the pure investor not to control. He is looking for an investment. He is very diffident about how he handles the proxies. He is diffident about getting too much control in the particular company, because consequences, legal consequences, flow from that. But at some point it may perhaps get beyond his power, because he has funds to invest and he may not find all of the avenues that he would seek. But I emphasize that I think at the present time it is still so small an element in the overall availability of securities that it has not become the problem that it might in the future.[8]

While Mr. McCloy may or may not have been correct in his assessment in 1955, the evidence indicates that the problem is one that exists today. First, if institutional investors are meeting their fiduciary responsibilities, they must make a substantial investment in research and time to make an investment in a company; the price of selling out cannot be measured solely against the costs of buying in. Second, while a single pension fund may limit itself to a small fraction of a corporation's voting stock, a large bank may administer and be responsible for the prudent investment of many such funds. Fractions added combine into large holdings. Third, the ability to move in and out of a corporation cannot be measured in terms of the corporation's outstanding shares of stock. That is obviously much too large a number. Rather, liquidity should be considered in relation to volume of sales or floating supply—a mere fraction of the amount outstanding. The latter point was illustrated by the case of *United States v. E. I. du Pont de Nemours and Company*.[9]

---

voting stocks of any one company should not exceed three-fourths of 1 percent of any company's voting stock. A higher percentage limitation of this type of investment may be established by any trustee or trustees, with the approval of the coordinator, provided that the investments of the combined trust funds in the voting stocks of any one company do not exceed 5 percent of such company's voting stock." *Hearings on S. Res. 40 Before the Subcommittee on Welfare and Pension Funds of the Senate Committee on Labor and Public Welfare*, 84th Cong., 1st Sess., pt. 3, at 1137 (1955).

[8] *Hearings on Factors Affecting the Buying and Selling of Equity Securities Before the Senate Committee on Banking and Currency*, 84th Cong., 1st Sess., at 442 (1955). In this connection, an official of a very powerful bank took great pains in telling one of the authors that "institutions just do not invest in the same stocks. There is little danger of us coming into a control position."

[9] 353 U.S. 586 (1957).

The Government in an antitrust action sought divestiture by du Pont of its interests in General Motors, which amounted to 23 per cent of the motor company's voting stock. An expert witness testified that an increase in General Motors stock of 10 per cent in the past resulted in a decline in price of approximately 5 per cent; an increase of 20 per cent brought a decline of between 10 and 15 per cent. Additional testimony emphasized the devastating effect that a 23 per cent increase in supply would have on the market. Divestiture, ruled out by the lower courts, was finally obtained, but only after two trips to the Supreme Court,[10] which twice set aside the findings of the trial court. At last an elaborate plan was developed and approved by the Government, calling for the distribution of GM shares to du Pont shareholders over a period of ten years. Even then the remedy was felt to be so harsh that special tax legislation was adopted to relieve the tax burden on thousands of innocent shareholders not parties to the case.

One final conclusion of fact is that institutional investors are in a position to obtain corporate information not available to other shareholders. This position springs from the power of large holdings and from the ability as a day-to-day matter to send competent men into the field to question management, not to mention the fact that institutions are themselves big business and, thus, their executives are the natural associates of industrial executives. Some would argue that the unfairness of institutional investors' receiving such information is tempered by the apathy of most individual shareholders in seeking corporate news, saying, in effect, that someone has to mind the corporate store. But the problem is not the mere receipt of corporate information but the use that is made of it, and the fact remains that institutional investors do receive information that allows them to exploit opportunities to the exclusion of other shareholders.

The conclusions of fact may be more generally summed up: Institutional investors possess power in their portfolio corporations. This power is reflected on the stock market as a factor in raising or lowering stock prices. It accordingly affects other shareholders. As this power mounts, institutions will experience increasing difficulty in liquidating their interests in a corporation. This will result

[10] United States v. E. I. du Pont de Nemours and Company, 366 U.S. 316 (1961).

from the practical economic limitations on the amount of stock the market can absorb and from the legal implications that spring from institutional control of portfolio corporations and the use of corporate information not available to the general public. Finally, this power, exercised or nonexercised, serves as a sanction or endorsement of management. The steady vote for management serves to perpetuate the professional managers. A vote against management could unseat them. The use or nonuse of the power is of vital import to other shareholders, for it can be of great weight in determining the course of their corporate interests. Some examples of the uses of this power are considered in the following chapter. Institutions have not always remained the silent partners in American businesses, despite the fact that they may have wished to do so.

4

᭡᭡᭡᭡᭡᭡᭡

SOME USES OF
INSTITUTIONAL
POWER

To the "Corporate Democrats" power is equated with the vote. The exercise of power must be measured by the exercise of the vote, and the facts show that institutional investors vote in accordance with the management position, and against independent shareholder proposals. The conclusion prompted is this: "[I]nvestment companies as shareholders are doing little or nothing toward fulfillment of their obligations as shareholder participants in corporate affairs, either to their own shareholders or to shareholders generally."[1] This conclusion, insofar as mutual funds are concerned, was fully borne out by the Wharton Report. On the face of it, institutional investors have pleaded guilty to this charge of "automatic" support of management. The reason given by the institutions is summarized by the so-called Wall Street Rule: "When we buy into a corporation we buy management. We, therefore, support management as long as we are in a corporation. If we don't like management, we sell."

[1] Emerson, *Some Sociological and Legal Aspects of Institutional and Individual Participation Under the SEC's Shareholder Proposal Rule*, 34 U. Det. L.J. 528 (1956).

For the most part, institutions are investors, not controllers. Professor Berle has written:

> There is ample evidence for the proposition that the institutional holders of common stock do not use, do not wish to use, the voting power of the stock they have accumulated. They do not get together to concert action. They do not as a rule enter into proxy fights. They almost invariably vote their stock for the management slate. When they seriously dislike the management of corporations in which they have holdings, their policy is to sell. Therefore, they say, "We cannot be considered part of the power pyramid," and they say it in all sincerity.[2]

This description of institutional action, of either quietly staying in or selling, is too clear-cut. It presents a black-and-white picture when reality consists of shades of grey. The prevailing view of institutional behavior should be reexamined. That view is founded, in part, on the assumption that it is a relatively simple and clear-cut matter for institutions to determine when they do and when they do not like management. But what if the institutional investor does not *seriously* dislike management? It simply disapproves of some act that may hurt but not destroy its investment. What if the institutional investor favors an act that management opposes, which it feels will strengthen an already good investment?

The prevailing view also assumes that institutional action will necessarily take the form of a vote in open forum. It precludes influence of another sort. It places a *sine qua non* on the standard "open covenants openly arrived at." It ignores the pressure that an informal conference with management might exert. An open meeting may tend to harden existing positions under the glare of publicity, while a less formal discussion permits compromise without fear of embarrassment. So, too, the prevailing view overlooks the stamp of approval that the mere fact of institutional holdings in a corporation may carry. Institutional ownership of securities may significantly influence corporate management, without exercise of voting power. The financial institutions represent an aggregate of well-informed and frequently aggressive investors in a position

[2] BERLE, POWER WITHOUT PROPERTY 55 (1959).

to judge management's performance. An investment trust, insurance company, or bank may make a very searching investigation of a company in which it is considering an investment. Indeed, it is obligated to do so. Such an investigation represents time, effort, and expense, and once an investment is made, liquidation necessarily represents a loss, unless at a substantially increased price.

Thus, to the extent that an institution can use its power over management to further its own investment objectives, it might reasonably be expected to do so. Some examples of the uses of institutional power may serve to illustrate.[3]

1. The story of Sewell Avery's rise and decline as the great leader of Montgomery Ward is familiar reading. When Louis E. Wolfson made his bid for control of the mighty mail order house in 1949, Avery was an old man no longer capable of running the company. His policies were outdated. Afraid of a postwar depression, Avery refused to expand the company. Rather, he tightened up, accumulated huge amounts of cash, and prepared for the worst, while the company's principal competitor grew. He slapped down suggestions for change from his directors with a heavy hand. George Whitney and Harry P. Davidson of J. P. Morgan & Company, the firm that persuaded Avery to lend his executive talents to Ward's in 1931, resigned from the board.

With a will to wrest control of the company, Wolfson began his battle. The object of his entreaties was the institutional investors with their large blocks of stock, the dominant shareholders of the mail order company. Would they vote for him?

Before Wolfson publicly fired the first salvo against the management of Montgomery Ward, he met privately with officials of at least one institution. An attempt to buy their stock was refused. "But tell us what your program for the company would be if you got control," institutional officials told him. "If we like it, we'll throw our votes to you." Wolfson explained, but they did not like what they heard. It seemed to the officials that Wolfson planned to liquidate part of the company and use the cash together with the large amount already in the corporate treasury for higher dividends or to obtain control of other companies. As far as they

[3] See generally LIVINGSTON, THE AMERICAN STOCKHOLDER (1958). The examples that follow are based on interviews conducted by one of the authors with officials of a number of institutions.

were concerned, that was not the way to build Montgomery Ward on a long-term basis. Further, even to carry out his avowed plan, they felt that the would-be challenger lacked a strong enough management team. Wolfson was not their man, but he provided the lever, which did not exist before, to push Avery out and bring a new management in.

Losing major institutional support, Wolfson opened the public phase of his battle. At that point the institutional investor referred to before received other visitors, some directors of Montgomery Ward. Confidently, the directors said, "We'll get your vote, won't we?" No, answered the officers of the institution. "The time has come to do something about Avery and you know it." The behind-the-scenes pressure that failed once before now brought results. The directors of Montgomery Ward agreed with the fund but would put nothing in writing. To do so would insure Wolfson's chances if their stand were ever "leaked" to the public. In addition, there was the personal reputation of Avery to consider. Nobody wanted to humiliate a man who had served well and had just grown old.

When the annual meeting came newspapermen gathered, waiting for angry shareholders to overthrow the rule of Avery. J. A. Livingston expressed the surprised reaction of most of the press at the meeting:

Alas, for expectations! Massachusetts Investors Trust quietly voted its stock for nominees other than Avery. A. Moyer Kulp, vice-president of Wellington, issued a statement before the meeting saying he was cumulating Wellington's vote for one director, David A. Crawford, president of Pullman Company. Vocal dissonance came solely from W. McNeil Kennedy, an attorney representing the Chicago investment counsel firm of Stein, Roe & Farnham. Kennedy protested against the "exodus of managerial talent, over forty in number, that had marched in and out of Montgomery Ward in the last few years." The Stein, Roe & Farnham stock wasn't voted at all.

After that the meeting fizzled like an improperly loaded firecracker. Some stockholders rose to praise Avery as the grand old man of Ward's. Of all nominees for director, Avery corralled the greatest number of votes. His own holdings, of course, could have been cumulated to that effect. Anyway, he was morally victorious. Most banks, trust companies, insurance companies, investment trusts and individual investors, large and small, went along with law, order, and the line of least resistance—Avery. . . . Ward was a comfortable, safe stock. And that, essentially, is what most investors want.[4]

The meeting, however, was not the end, just as it was not the beginning. Avery was elected only to resign. Had the directors made a deal with the institutional holders?

The Senate committee investigating the stock market in 1955 attempted to draw the answer from John A. Barr, the new chairman of the board and president of Montgomery Ward Company. Senator Lehman asked Mr. Barr whether he "could tell us the reason why Mr. Avery resigned as president in view particularly of the fact I should imagine most of the stockholders who voted their stock at the meeting thought he was going to continue as president."

> Mr. Barr: I think that I cannot answer your question as to why he resigned. I think it is quite speculative for any man to attempt to state the reasons for another man's action. Neither do I know that it is a fact that most of the stockholders who voted for the management slate expected that Mr. Avery would continue in his position as chairman of the board for the ensuing year.

When Senator Lehman began more intensive questioning of Mr. Barr to determine if Avery had been asked to resign, the answers given were tightly qualified:

> Senator Lehman: Was there any pressure brought to bear on Mr. Avery to resign as chairman of the board?
> Mr. Barr: I do not know. So far as I am concerned, I did not bring any pressure on him.
> Senator Lehman: Do you know of any?
> Mr. Barr: I can speak for myself.
> Senator Lehman: You do not know whether pressure was brought to bear on him?
> Mr. Barr: No. I do not.[5]

The company once again launched a program of expansion.

[4] LIVINGSTON, THE AMERICAN STOCKHOLDER 152-53 (1955).
[5] *Hearings on S. 879 Before a Subcommittee of the Senate Committee on Banking and Currency,* 84th Cong., 1st Sess., pt. 3, at 1339 (1956).

The reservoir of capital so attractive to Wolfson was put to work. The means for achieving the end, according to the official of the institution who related the story, was discussion, backed by the power of the vote. The end, of course, was arrived at by making a value judgment as to what man and what policies would best serve the company. and thus the institution's investment.

But, significantly, the method employed for achieving that end was not an expensive, drawn-out proxy fight, either to unseat Avery or to insure that Wolfson did not gain control. Institutional power, perhaps long dormant, was ultimately forced to exert itself in order to preserve a valued investment.

2. As an investment, the New York Central Railroad was generally not favored in 1954 by institutional investors. The Central was engaged in a battle to stay on the black side of the ledger. To aid in the struggle, management, led by William White, curtailed the dividend. To institutional investors, the inability to pay dividends was only one additional piece of evidence of a sick company. The stock that institutions never purchased, and perhaps some they sold, found its way into the hands of speculators and the late Robert Young. Without a powerful block of institutional votes to insure their power, management became more susceptible to attack. That attack came in 1954. Young and his allies made their bid for control and won. J. A. Livingston, the financial editor of the *Philadelphia Bulletin,* and an observer of the proxy contest, wrote:

> White had been beaten because he was . . . the kind of person who could not conduct a campaign to appeal to speculators. Young, on the other hand, had political flair. He made his pitch to the large group of traders and speculators who had bought Central for a market advance, who had not even troubled to have the Central stock transferred. They left the shares in brokers' names. The statistics bear this out.
>
> Stock in brokers' names went for Young by a two-to-one margin—1,372,000 shares to 678,000, including the 200,000 shares owned by Young and Kirby. . . . White got a majority from stockholders who had registered the stock in their own names. These are persons who might be described as long-term investors.[6]

[6] *Supra* note 3, at 140.

It is not our purpose to pass on the merits of the Young-White controversy. That we shall leave to history. But there are lessons to be drawn from the Central episode in terms of the exercise of institutional power. First, management was denied a block of institutional votes that might have aided in either thwarting aspirations of a contest or in insuring victory once one took place. Approximately 90 per cent of the institutional votes available were cast for White. The denial of an institutional bloc of votes sufficient to insure reelection was a theme of Mr. Livingston when he analyzed the difference between the Montgomery Ward and the New York Central fights. Second, a proxy fight tends to cloud real issues and to highlight personalities. Management, as well as the challengers, finds that the war must be waged with emotion rather than reason. The man with the brighter smile rather than the man with the most ability might thus emerge the victor. The calm objectivity of an institutional investor is lacking.

In Senate Hearings in 1955, J. Sinclair Armstrong, then Chairman of the Securities and Exchange Commission, introduced a report on proxy fights published by the American Institute of Management. The report stated, in part:

> "[T]he [investment] funds are now the most significant single group of investors in the land. As such, their responsibility for overseeing the management of the companies in which their shareholders' funds are invested is not one which can continue to be shirked. Their unique position imposes inescapable obligations upon them. It is our judgment that they must meet these obligations when vital issues face companies whose stock they hold.
>
> The alternative, it is now apparent, is for no effective voice to be raised against mismanagement in time for constructive action to be taken in a thoroughly responsible way by thoroughly responsible men. The door's opened to adventurers who, seizing upon discontent, strive for control over the assets and lives of thousands.
>
> Contests so generated exploit without correcting defects in management or in corporate policies. They seize upon shortcomings, not to secure a remedy, but to attract support for purported correctives which, in fact, are mere bait upon a

proxy hook. Their purpose is self-enrichment and the enlarge-
ment of personal power.[7]

3. It was with a sense of pride that an official of a major life
insurance company described how industry had been taught to
save through direct borrowing from insurance companies. While
at one time many industrial concerns distributed much of their
profit in dividends, they now commonly retain substantial sums.
This policy is partly traceable to the demands of life insurance
companies to provide added security for their loans. *Prima facie,*
this might seem detrimental to the shareholders, but on closer
analysis it is often for their benefit. In a sense, it is a question of
whether the corporation can make a larger return on the funds
than the shareholder could, after paying the dividend tax, for
retained earnings provide funds for research and experimentation,
costly risks that must be taken if the company is to advance. No
recitation of facts is needed to demonstrate the economic importance of research. Competition today is to a large extent competition in technology: "Internally accumulated capital is risk capital
par excellence. It goes into the treasuries of the corporations; it
is at the disposal of the managements of those corporations; it is
precisely in the hands of enterprises which have already carried out
risk operations—and have succeeded."[8]

Thus, the influence of institutional power is not confined to
approval or disapproval of particular corporate activities. Institutions can be, and in fact have been, instrumental in the shaping
of fundamental corporate policies. The role of insurance companies
in the private placements by corporations of their senior securities
has already been discussed. There can be little doubt that the
restrictions imposed by insurance company loan agreements on
essentially internal corporate activities have contributed substantially to the development of sound policies of corporate finance and
planning. The enforced retention of adequate capital reserves and
the limitations on capital expenditures, mortgaging of corporate
property, and long-term commitments, without the approval of the

[7] *Supra* note 5, at 1528. The SEC has adopted rules to curtail unfounded
charges of the type that were common in the great proxy fights of the postwar
years. Rule 14a-11 under the Securities Exchange Act of 1934, 17 C.F.R.
§ 240.14a-11.
[8] *Supra* note 2, at 47.

investing insurance company, are commonly accepted as part of the price that must be paid to obtain insurance company financing. The results, on the whole, have been generally favorable, not only for the insurance companies seeking maximum security for their investments but for their portfolio companies as well.

4. "Excessive" executive compensation has often been a favorite target for the Corporate Democrats. Information relating to salaries and stock options, required to be published in the corporation's annual proxy statement, is relatively easy to obtain. Indeed, the Corporate Democrats claim some success in forcing down executive compensation. One of the victories they claim is the reduction of top-management compensation at Bethlehem Steel.[9] To the institutional investors, however, executive compensation becomes a subject to act upon only when its excessiveness is reflected (1) in substantially reducing company profits (which is rare), (2) in giving rise to labor-management problems,[10] and (3) in creating a tone of corporate extravagance. Therefore, it is not often that institutional investors move in the area of compensation. But

[9] Wall Street Journal, June 17, 1959, p. 26, col. 2.

[10] This charge was made in *Hearings on S. 215 Before the Subcommittee on Antitrust and Monopoly of the Senate Committee on the Judiciary*, 86th Cong., 1st Sess., pt. 11 (1959). The charge was formalized in a Senate report, Subcomm. on Antitrust and Monopoly of the Senate Comm. on the Judiciary, *Study of Administered Prices in the Steel Industry*, S. REP. No. 1387, 85th Cong., 2d Sess. 107 (1958): "Executive salaries in the industrial corporations are only a small proportion of the total wages and salary bill so that the direct effect of changes in such compensation can only be negligible. Their indirect effects can be disturbing, however. An average compensation to each officer-director in a steel company of $468,000 in 1 year acts as a challenge, a red flag, to labor unions and individual laborers to seek all they can. And, it is difficult to persuade labor to hold a wage line when it knows the generous manner in which officer-directors compensate themselves."

A graphic example can be taken from a recent steel strike. In a full-page advertisement the union ran a headline stating "How the chief executive of one of the major steel companies benefits personally, while Steelworkers' families suffer the hardships of a shut-down." After describing the terms of a stock option the union declared: "This is in addition to his salary, pension, apartments, clubs, airplanes, railroad cars and unlimited expenses he may use for personal luxuries plus any special bonus deal, or post employment benefit he may have. And 19 of the top 22 Steel Companies have stock option plans similar to the one above. Little wonder that these executives want to 'hold the line' on wages. Their personal profits and stock equities will rise even further.

"Their arrogance, greed, and desire for personal gain would make old-time 'steel barons' blush with envy." N.Y. Times, Aug. 7, 1959, p. 13.

there are times. Institutional investors have told of company officials who, without any apparent justification, bestowed upon themselves ever-higher salaries, deferred compensation plans, and stock options. A telephone call, followed by a visit with management, may be enough to curb an inflated appetite. The calls may ask for an explanation for the increases and, when one cannot be given, may suggest that the compensation be "adjusted."[11] While this sort of institutional action is rare, doubtless the knowledge that it can happen has a prophylactic effect.

Of course, executive compensation is an extremely sensitive subject and a kind of community of interest may understandably make institutional executives reluctant to complain about salaries paid to their brother executives of portfolio companies. Again, insurance companies have probably exercised a healthy restraining influence. Insurance company loan agreements sometimes limit executive compensation, at least at the approximate levels existing at the time the loan is made.

5. An insurgent group of shareholders were anxious to merge one banking institution with another. The directors of Bank A opposed the merger. The insurgents, realizing they could not defeat the board in a proxy contest, nevertheless sought the assistance of institutional investors in seating as large a minority as possible. In discussions, one institutional investor took the position, which was accepted, that it would support a "watchdog" group of two insurgent directors, but no more. Additional directors would disrupt the operations of the board and interfere with business.

Of course, it is common practice for institutions to be represented on the boards of directors of the country's largest corporations, although, whether or not they could properly be termed "watchdog" directors is doubtful. For example, George Champion, the chairman of the board of the Chase Manhattan Bank, is a director of American Smelting and Refining Company; J. Victor Herd, chairman of the boards of the Continental Insurance Companies, Henry T. Heald, president of the Ford Foundation, and Floyd D. Brace, chairman of the board of The First National Bank of Boston, are all directors of AT&T; Harold H. Helm, chairman

---

[11] Three such cases were related in interviews by one of the authors with officials of institutional investors.

of Chemical Bank New York Trust Company, is a director of Bethlehem Steel; Robert E. McNeill, chairman of Manufacturers Hanover Trust Company, is a director of Union Carbide Corporation. A recent study by a House committee headed by Representative Emanuel Celler found that the directors of General Motors hold management positions in thirty-two industrial and commercial corporations, twenty-two banks and other financial institutions (including Morgan Guaranty Trust Company, the nation's sixth largest bank), and four insurance companies. The same study found that the directors of General Electric hold management posts in forty-five other industrial and commercial companies, seventeen banks and financial institutions, and twelve insurance companies. Directors of the First National City Bank of New York were found to serve on the boards of eight of the country's largest industrial corporations, including Jersey Standard, U.S. Steel, Ford, Westinghouse, G.E., and Standard of California.

The Supreme Court recently had occasion to pass on one aspect of institutional representation on the boards of large corporations. In *Blau v. Lehman*,[12] a partner of Lehman Brothers, one of the nation's largest investment banking concerns, was a director of Tidewater Oil Company. The partnership purchased and sold shares of Tidewater within a period of less than six months and a stockholder sued on behalf of Tidewater to recover the "short swing" profit made by Lehman Brothers under section 16(b) of the Securities Exchange Act of 1934. The SEC joined in the suit, as a friend of the court, asserting that the stockholder should be able to recover on behalf of Tidewater the entire partnership profit, not just the partner-director's proportionate share of those profits as determined by the partnership agreement. To hold otherwise, the SEC argued, would open the door for the great Wall Street trading firms to reap huge profits from insider trading by merely giving up the share of those profits allocable to the particular partner-director. But the Court held that the firm itself was not a "director" and thus could not be considered an "insider" unless the stockholder could show either that one of the firm's partners had been "deputed" to serve on the board as its representative, or that the firm had actually received and acted upon inside information in

[12] 368 U.S. 403 (1962).

effecting the "short swing" transaction. Since neither of these could be proved, recovery was limited to the individual partner's proportionate share of the profits.

Justice Douglas (a former chairman of the SEC) and the Chief Justice dissented, quoting Brandeis' description of corporate directorships as a "happy hunting ground" for investment bankers: "The goose that lays golden eggs has been considered a most profitable possession. But even more profitable is the privilege of taking the golden eggs laid by somebody else's goose. The investment bankers and their associates now enjoy that privilege."[13]

6. Institutions had large holdings in Company A. The company had a policy of raising needed capital by the public offering of convertible debentures. To some institutions the effect of this policy diluted their equity. They pointed this out in discussions with officers of Company A. They showed how Company B raised needed capital by increasing its fixed debt and, therefore, maintained stock equity. The pressure brought to bear was of no avail. Company A held to its policy. The price paid was that some institutions liquidated their holdings in A and purchased B.

At first blush, it might appear that management could hardly be concerned whether an institution buys or sells shares of its company. While this sometimes may be true, it is often important to management, if not to obtain institutional shareholders, at least to keep those it has. Institutional market activity, as we have seen, can have major impact on the market price of stocks. This influence can depress the market, as well as raise it. In addition, institutions, with their lower turnover rate, may tend to "take up the slack" in times when the shares of a particular company are temporarily out of favor with the public. And the market price of the company's shares is a matter of concern to management, from the standpoint of overall public relations, as well as the potential implication that the company is being run successfully.

Perhaps more importantly, executive stock options have become an important supplement to management compensation, largely because of the more favorable capital gains tax treatment they receive. However, in order to qualify for this tax advantage, the Internal Revenue Code provides that options must be exercisable

[13] *Id.* at 419.

at no less than 100 per cent of the market price for the shares on the date the option was granted. Thus, an option is of little value unless the market price of the company's shares substantially increases in value.

7. The vote is an ultimate and usually cumbersome weapon. Institutions do not like to use it. Yet, if they are pressed hard enough, and if they find it to their disadvantage to sell, they will use the ballot. Robert W. Ladd, the secretary of Massachusetts Investors Growth Stock Fund, wrote of the Fund's activity in 1958: "As far as Massachusetts Investors Trust is concerned, and which Fund is also managed from this office, that Trust voted against a portfolio company's recommendation on retirement income, and voted against the management of two portfolio companies in connection with mergers."[14] Similarly, Edward A. Merkel, the president of Madison Fund, a closed-end investment company, was quoted by Gilbert as saying:

> When we see an abuse in a company in which we are a substantial stockholder, we make an all out effort to needle the management to do the right thing. If this does not work, we will vote against management, whether or not there is a proxy fight. No matter what, we will at all times vote our stock. To do otherwise is in effect to disenfranchise our own shareholders and to default on one of our chief management obligations. And taking the easy way out by just disposing of our holding is to contradict the first principle of proper corporate practice.[15]

The Wharton Report found that while open-end companies seldom exercised a controlling influence over portfolio concerns, on several occasions they voted against management stock option plans and opposed other corporate action that would be disadvantageous to them and other stockholders.

Institutional investors clearly have the competence and the power to check corporate management in the area of corporate policy. Under certain conditions, that power is invoked. Even the nonexercise of power, as it is defined by the institutions, influences the course of corporate affairs and, more specifically, the interests

[14] Gilbert, 19th Annual Report of Stockholder Activities at Corporation Meetings During 1958, at 210.
[15] *Ibid.* at 202.

of other shareholders. The institutional investor would prefer to move quietly, unnoticed on the corporate scene, but more and more this is becoming impossible. Power carries with it responsibility. Mr. McCloy in 1955 might have attempted to avoid that responsibility by minimizing the power. Today he could not. In 1958 David Rockefeller, then vice chairman of the board of directors of The Chase Manhattan Bank, stated:

> I might . . . draw your attention to one important change in savings that *is* occurring: namely, the tendency for personal savings to flow more and more through institutions—through insurance companies, pension funds, mutual funds and the like—rather than through individual savings accounts. During the 'Sixties, corporations will find themselves dealing increasingly with these sophisticated investors. Moreover, I suspect that such investors will become more demanding of management as time moves on—that as holdings expand, institutions, as well as individuals, will feel obliged to take more active interest in seeing that corporations do indeed have good managements. This will be true especially if their holdings become so large that they cannot readily or quickly liquidate their investments, as is now their practice when they become dissatisfied with the management of a corporation in which they hold shares.[16]

[16] Address by David Rockefeller, "Business Enterprise and the Economy in the Next Ten Years," before the Special Conference for Financial Executives of the American Management Association at the Roosevelt Hotel, New York City, October 14, 1959 (Mimeo) at pp. 4-5.

5

〓〓〓〓〓〓〓

PRESENT LEGAL
RESTRAINTS ON THE USES
OF INSTITUTIONAL POWER

The accumulation of power by any political or economic group is a phenomenon to be watched. In the words of Lord Acton, "Power tends to corrupt; absolute power corrupts absolutely." It cannot be said that institutional investors, even as a group, have anything approaching absolute power in the sense of capacity to *control* either the stock market or the managements of their portfolio concerns. But this is not to say that institutions cannot *influence* trading and, for that matter, the managements of their portfolio corporations.

Institutional power is, of course, the object of practical as well as legal restraints. Surrounding the institutions are the daily competing economic and social pressures as well as a complex of state and federal statutes, regulations, administrative decisions, policies, and practices. Yet the institutions have learned to live with these forces, many of which are now of long standing. While the regulation of investment companies came more than a quarter of a century after the income tax, state supervision of life insurance companies had its beginnings at the turn of the nineteenth century, a hundred years before the revelations of the Armstrong Investigation, which rocked the entire industry.

Institutional investors may well be the natural objects of the heaviest of bureaucratic burdens that must be carried in modern society. Of this the institutions are the first to remind us. Recalling the dire predictions of Wall Street during the congressional hearings that led to the Securities Act of 1933 and the Securities Exchange Act of 1934, it is a wonder that the financial community, so burdened, could be so long a-dying, and look so healthy doing it. The fact of the matter is that regulation for the most part has been the salvation of the industry, as well as the economy, and this most industrial leaders now admit.

Our purpose now is to examine the framework of existing legal restraints on the exercise of institutional power. We do not, of course, attempt to describe in detail the labyrinth of laws, regulations, and administrative practices governing institutional behavior, but only those which seem most relevant to the problem of portfolio holdings.

Certain conclusions spring from that which follows. The form of regulation over institutional investors may vary. For banks federal government plays a greater role than state government, while the opposite is true for the insurance industry. The substance of regulation as applied by the specialized agencies is nevertheless the same: protection of assets, security for the depositor or the insured.

Save for the antitrust laws, the regulators have evidenced little or no concern over the activities of institutional investors in relation to their portfolio corporations. The reasons for this are many: An agency may be denied funds necessary to understand and cope with emerging problems. Or the regulators may, to some extent, be captives of the regulated. Or the statutory authority for acting might either be lacking or in doubt.

Finally, the sorry fact also emerging from the description in this chapter is that most of the regulatory bodies have a difficult enough time achieving even the limited goals they pursue. It is highly questionable whether they are now prepared to assume new and substantially different responsibilities.

LIFE INSURANCE COMPANIES

It is not without reason that our discussion of the insurance industry centers around the life insurance companies, rather than the fire and casualty companies.

The life insurance business involves a far greater accumulation of assets than does any other line of insurance. The basic reason for this can be stated in many ways. Perhaps most simply, it is a matter of life insurance indemnifying against something which is sure to happen (i.e., death) rather than against something which probably will not happen (e.g., the destruction of a building by fire within a given year). The feature of asset accumulation gives rise to the necessity for regulation of types of investment, valuation of assets, and dividend practices.

The other distinguishing feature of life insurance, from the point of view of regulation, is the great number of years over which the contract extends. It may be reasonably safe to base this year's casualty premiums on last year's losses and expenses, but this year's life insurance premiums must be calculated on estimates of mortality, investment, and operating expense for the life of the insured and perhaps also for the lives of one or two generations of beneficiaries. It is chiefly this very long time span of life insurance obligations which creates the necessity for the actuarial science, and for government regulation in the areas of mortality tables, interest assumptions, and the long term adequacy of policy reserves.[1]

Thus, among the oldest of institutional investors in the nation are the life insurance companies. As early as 1794 there is recorded the grant of a charter to the Insurance Company of North America, and in the same charter is recorded the condition that the company set up reserves for possible losses.[2] Just a year later the Massachusetts legislature allowed incorporation of an insurance company with the proviso that it invest only in government obligations. From the beginning, safety, the conservation of assets, was the principal factor of concern to the state. It was only logical when a few years later the states made the first moves toward overseeing the internal affairs of the insurance companies. "In 1807 Massachusetts enacted the first general provision which required every domestic insurance company to file with the legislature a statement of its affairs. This was the forerunner of the modern requirement for filing with the insur-

---

[1] Dineen, Procter & Gardners, *The Economics and Principles of Insurance Supervision,* in 2 INSURANCE AND GOVERNMENT 21 (U. Wis. Insurance Series No. 1, 1960) [hereinafter referred to as "Insurance Series"].

[2] LINCOLN, INSURANCE SUPERVISION, Symposium on Life Insurance: Trends and Problems, the S.S. Huebner Foundation for Insurance Education Lectures, University of Pennsylvania, 8, 10 (1943). Mr. Lincoln was President of the Metropolitan Life Ins. Co.

ance commissioner a complete annual statement."[3] There then followed the broad supervisory delegation of power to an administrative agency specially designated to observe the operations of these companies:

> Modern supervision had its beginning when New Hampshire in 1851 established the first independent Board of Insurance Commissioners, consisting of three members who devoted their full time to their task. The statute imposed upon them the duty to examine each year into the affairs of each insurance company and to report to the legislature. . . . In the meantime New York, however, had, in 1859, created the office of Superintendent of Insurance, the first independent and single-headed administrative office in the United States charged with the duty of supervising the business of insurance.[4]

Control by the state, to the exclusion of the federal government, continued until 1944 when the Supreme Court, reversing a line of prior cases, ruled that insurance is subject to the Commerce Clause of the Constitution.[5] No sooner was this done, however, than Congress relinquished to the states much of its jurisdiction over the insurance industry.[6] Whatever logic might dictate, the historical development of state regulation was too far along to turn back then.

The inquisitorial and visitorial powers of the insurance superintendent are today the states' most vital powers over the insurance industry. Using New York as an illustration, consider the requirement of an annual report that each insurer must file with the superintendent. No set list of items is provided by the statute. The superintendent may establish the form and content of the report. The means are in his hands to obtain full disclosure of each insurer's financial condition.[7] Nor does the inquisitorial power end here. The superintendent may specially question and demand answers from any insurer "in relation to its transactions or condition or any matter connected therewith."[8]

[3] *Ibid.*
[4] *Id.* at 11.
[5] United States v. South-Eastern Underwriters Assn., 322 U.S. 533 (1944).
[6] McCarran-Ferguson Act, 59 Stat. 33, March 9, 1945, 15 U.S.C. §§ 1011-15.
[7] N.Y. Insurance Law § 26.
[8] *Id.* § 27.

Finally, the superintendent has been given the right of visitation. Every three years he must exercise this right in making an examination of every life insurance company licensed to do business in the state. To make the triennial examination of the affairs of a large insurance company may consume the full time of a staff of investigators for a year and a half.[9] The purpose of the report goes beyond the mere counting of company assets. It is intended to determine whether the company can meet present and future obligations.[10] When the industry is not undergoing the three-year inspection or receiving interrogatories, it may be subjected to an on-the-spot investigation by the superintendent without cause having to be shown.[11] Further, the superintendent need not, and in most cases does not, give notice or a hearing before such an examination is conducted. A suspected company must be taken by surprise, lest it juggle or transfer its assets, as has been done in one or two instances, according to insurance department officials.

The impact of visitation on an industry to which the public is so sensitive can cause that industry much damage. Indeed, the threat of visitation has been used at times to accomplish objects not authorized by statute. Consider this example: Insurance commissioners had been investigating the settlement of health and accident claims of certain companies. Some concerns not investigated "poached upon the agency forces of companies already examined, by pointing out to the agents the undesirable publicity, which the examined companies had received, and thus inducing the agents to transfer their affiliations and many of their customers to the company not yet examined."[12] By resolution the Convention of Insurance Commissioners in 1911 declared with but one voice raised in opposition that "such company so poaching will be immediately examined and full publicity given to the facts."[13] Commenting on the resolution, one author wrote:

When it is borne in mind that no state has, or had then, a

[9] *Id.* § 28(2)(a).

[10] Conklin, *Institutional Size—Life Insurance*, 17 LAW & CONTEMP. PROB. 219, 237 (1952).

[11] N.Y. Insurance Law § 28(1).

[12] PATTERSON, THE INSURANCE COMMISSIONER IN THE UNITED STATES 352, 353 (1927).

[13] *Id.* at 352.

statute making it unlawful to "poach" another company's solic-
itors, it is obvious that the power of examination may be used
to enforce a commissioner's ideas of what the conduct of a company ought to be, even though there would be no statutory
ground for revocation of the company's license.[14]

The judiciary has endeavored to preserve the vitality of visitation;
few bars have been placed on the use of it. Courts are inclined to a
"broad and liberal construction of the statutes defining the inquisitorial powers and rights of the commissioner."[15]
The potential powers of the superintendent of any state are
amplified by the uniformity of regulation and the extraterritorial
effect of some states' laws.

[A]n insurance company domiciled, say in Iowa, and wishing
to conduct business in another state must conform substantially
to the regulatory standards of that state. In this way, especially
for those companies doing business on a nationwide basis, the
regulations of the strictest states tend to govern. New York
State insurance law has had wide influence in this respect, since
companies doing business in New York hold well over four
fifths of all United States companies' assets.[16]

Effectiveness of State Regulation of Insurance. Professor
Orfield has written:

The principal objects of governmental regulation of insurance
should be solvency, fair practices, and competent service. . . .
The greatest of these is solvency. The ability of an insurer to
meet its obligations depends on its financial condition. In turn,
its financial condition depends on sound investments, accurate
estimates of liabilities and unforeseen contingencies. The statutes of the leading insurance states have set high standards.
The state insurance departments have done excellent work in
enforcing these standards through systems of reports, examinations, audits and regulations.[17]

[14] *Ibid.*
[15] Metropolitan Life Insurance Company v. Clay, 164 S.W. 968 (Ky. 1914).
[16] *Supra* note 10 at 237.
[17] Orfield, *Improving State Regulation of Insurance,* 32 MINN. L. REV. 219,
244 (1948).

Through the National Association of Insurance Commissioners (NAIC), an organization more than ninety years old, has come uniformity and ever increasing effectiveness in each state's ability to administer the laws relating to the life insurance industry.[18] By way of example, the NAIC Committee on Examinations has divided the nation into six "zones," each containing approximately eight states. Whenever an examination of a company is undertaken by officials in the state where a company has its home or central office, the NAIC is notified so that the examination can be extended to other zones where the company has substantial operations.

Yet, for all that NAIC may do, effective regulation depends ultimately on the capacity of a state's office of insurance superintendent. It might be said that there are three principal factors that go to make up capacity: (1) the ability and experience of the superintendent and his staff, (2) the funds necessary to do the job, and (3) the willingness to regulate. Information relating to each of these elements was gathered as recently as 1960 by the Subcommittee on Antitrust and Monopoly of the Senate Judiciary Committee in a special study of state insurance regulation.[19]

[18] Insurance Series No. 1 at 10: "The NAIC now has to its credit a long list of legislative and administrative solutions of major problems facing the insurance industry—solutions which the NAIC, often with industry assistance, has designed and for which it has now more or less nationwide acceptance. As a result of the great lack of uniformity in the market values used by the different insurance companies upon the securities scheduled in their annual statements to insurance departments, the NAIC created in 1907 its Valuations Committee. As stated in the NAIC Proceeding of 1907: " 'That it is the sense of this convention that some plan should be adopted and arrangements made, if possible, for obtaining, in the promptest and most feasible way, uniformity in the market values of stocks and bonds held by the insurance companies. . . .' This helped the industry to weather sharp market declines in 1907, 1912, 1917 and 1929, and still provides much-needed stability of treatment of asset valuation problems. In 1941 and 1958 the NAIC was the most important single factor in achieving an orderly and substantially simultaneous shift to more modern mortality tables. In the crisis following the S.E.U.A. decision, an NAIC committee drafted the prototype used by Congress as the basis for U.S. Public Law 15. It provided invaluable help by drafting and securing state-by-state passage of a State Fair Trade Practices Act, a necessity if state regulation was to be preserved. Recent examples of the usefulness of its role have been its successful sponsorship of the 1950 Uniform Accident and Sickness Policy Provisions Law and the Credit Insurance Model Bill."

[19] Senate Judiciary Committee, *The Insurance Industry*, S. REP. No. 1834, 86th Cong., 2d Sess. (1960) [hereinafter referred to as *Insurance Industry Report*]. The report's findings were rooted primarily in answers received from

The subcommittee's findings were not encouraging. Few of the superintendents had backgrounds that prepared them for their duties. Of fifty-two insurance commissioners, twenty-nine indicated that they had specific professional qualifications before taking office. One reason for the lack of professionalism is the low rate of compensation. Only seven states paid their insurance chiefs $15,000 or more annually: California, $17,000; Florida, $17,500; Louisiana, $16,000; New Jersey, $18,000; New York, $18,500; Pennsylvania, $15,000; Texas, $20,000.

"In addition to the question of compensating insurance commissioners, the position to which commissioners migrate after leaving office also is important. In the data submitted by the various states on this subject, it appears that out of a total of 95 persons who were formerly insurance commissioners and who are now presently employed, 37 of them are now employed or working in the insurance industry."[20] This, of course, is quite significant as it indicates that one of the indirect compensations of the office is the possibility of subsequent employment in the insurance industry.

The difficulties encountered in providing effective departmental leadership are compounded in shaping an efficient staff, which is so vital to meaningful regulation.

[A]ll States have recognized that the work of insurance supervision has outgrown the capacity of a single individual and have provided for one or more assistants such as actuaries, examiners, lawyers, clerks, and raters. In reviewing regulatory activities of the department, it must be kept in mind that the administrative staff of the department plays an important role in actually administering the State laws and must oppose the best talent the insurance industry can hire in disputes on rate filings, policy forms, trade practices, and financial activities. The technical skills and quality of the departmental staff are a key link in the armor of the department for protecting the public interest. Both sufficient quantity and quality of personnel are involved in the staffing problems.[21]

---

written interrogatories sent the several states. It was in large part this fact that constituted grounds for attacking the report's conclusions. (See the individual views of Senator Wiley at 248 and Senators Dirksen and Hruska at 258.)

[20] *Id.* at 130-31.
[21] *Id.* at 136.

The Senate subcommittee found that many departments are seriously understaffed and often are paying salaries that are grossly inadequate to attract and keep capable personnel. For example, actuaries, a highly professional group, are essential to the regulation of the life insurance industry. Yet fifteen states neither employed nor consulted with any in the administration of their insurance departments. Although insurance supervision involves frequent problems of interpretation of complex statutes, nineteen states employed no attorneys and only three of these states regularly consulted the state's attorney general regarding legal questions.[22]

Insurance departments are financed through premium taxes on the regulated. The yield from these levies is substantial. To take but a few illustrations, for 1957 New York collected more than $54 million in premium taxes; Illinois, $24 million; and Indiana, $8.5 million. Yet of these totals New York State, the acknowledged leader in insurance regulation, spent but $4.3 million on its insurance department for 1957; Illinois, $864,000; and Indiana, $181,000. For the entire nation it was found that $395 million was collected through the premium tax and of this only $16.9 million was expended for regulation.

Inadequate financing of the regulatory agencies was evidenced in the salaries paid employees. Compared to salaried attorneys in the nation for 1954, whose mean salary was $10,381, attorneys employed by state insurance departments for 1957 had a mean salary of $7,270. Similar statistics reflect the salary variations of actuaries, examiners, and rate technicians.

The Senate subcommittee studying life insurance concluded:

> [T]he qualifications established for selecting staff for insurance departments appear adequate and reasonable in terms of the

---

[22] *Ibid.* Perhaps the most dangerous situation, however, relates to the payment of the insurance examiner. "It is significant that 19 States indicated they allowed the insurance company being examined to pay the examiner directly. This appears as a highly questionable practice, in view of the fact that the company which is being examined is allowed to compensate directly the persons conducting the examination process and could influence their findings. The system itself creates grave conflict of interest problems. It has been reported to this subcommittee that some examiners have deliberately prolonged their investigations in order to receive this extra compensation upon the belief that a favorable report would overcome company objections as to the cost." *Id.* at 150.

jobs to be filled. However, it is highly doubtful whether personnel actually *meeting* these qualifications are hired by insurance departments, in view of the poor salaries which are paid. The insurance industry competes for much of the same talent required for adequate supervision and, therefore, to strengthen State supervision, it would appear that a much more realistic salary structure is in order.[23]

Recognizing the limitations of any regulatory program, we now come to the direction of insurance regulation, the substantive thrust of agency enforcement. Solvency, it will be recalled, should be the principal object of regulation. Yet, if this is so, limitations necessarily are placed on competition among insurers. Thus, in theory we cannot allow excessive rate battles; nor, it follows, can we permit speculative investments—for the loser in any competitive struggle, especially among mutual companies, is likely to be the policyholder.

So it is that many states have rigid rate regulations as well as high capital and surplus requirements. Yet, if these standards are too high, such competition as might exist is unnecessarily reduced. Specifically, one insurer may offer greater service than another, or effect savings in overhead that might be reflected in lower rates. The Senate subcommittee found:

> With the advent of multiple line policies which involve packaging several lines of an integrated contract many States have found that small companies are unable to meet the capital and surplus requirements to write these contracts. The result has been that competition from small companies in the package contract field is seriously curtailed in many States. This has alarming connotations to the future market structure of insurance since it may produce more concentration, merger activity, and hasten the demise of the small company. If multiple line underwriting represents the future development of the industry, insurance commissioners must be especially vigilant to preserve the vigor of competition by encouraging competent, small well-managed companies. Small companies should not be allowed to undertake risks they are incapable of handling, however. Too

---

[23] *Id.* at 142.

low minimums hardly seem justified in the interests of sound and efficient insurance supervision.[24]

In their concern for solvency, the states have omitted passing upon the competitive impact of mergers. Of course, mergers among small companies are one method of strengthening the financial condition of the newly formed enterprises. But consider the price paid. From 1953 to 1957 a total of 187 insurance mergers occurred.

> It is significant that in not one case did the State insurance departments refuse permission to merge or institute proceedings to prohibit a merger. Also, several States indicated that the merger question was not considered at all by the department, either with respect to approval or denial of permission to merge. These facts are significant in that one of the threats to a free competitive market in insurance is the extent to which merger activity is privileged or condoned either because of the lack of adequate State legislation or lack of concern with this problem. Furthermore, the interstate character of insurance also underscores the difficulties that insurance departments have with reference to the merger question. Two companies organized outside a given State may merge and not substantially affect the competitive market within their domiciliary States where they have sought approval for the merger. However, in the State where they do business as foreign companies, the competitive situation might be quite seriously affected and the local insurance commissioner in most cases would have virtually no jurisdiction or power to prevent the merger.[25]

While admitting the priority given to considerations of solvency, some state insurance laws contain provisions designed to encourage competition. New York, for example, has empowered its insurance superintendent to stop unfair methods of competition,[26] and the state attorney general is authorized to bring criminal proceedings against any insurance company violating the state antitrust laws. Indeed, all fifty states, following recommendations of an All-Industry Committee of NAIC, have adopted legislation prohibiting

[24] *Id.* at 212.
[25] *Id.* at 216-17.
[26] N.Y. Insurance Law §§ 274, 276.

specific unfair practices and condemning generally "other unfair competition, acts, and practices."[27]

The limitations, however, of inadequate appropriations have rendered this phase of insurance regulation impotent. From 1953 to 1957 not one of 201 license suspensions or revocations was rooted in an unfair trade practice charge. Moreover, in thirty states no formal action whatever was taken during the same time period for unfair trade practices.

> In only 10 states . . . was it possible to deduce that formal ac-
> tion had been taken against companies in violation of these
> statutes. New York leads the list with 83 such actions or over
> one-third of all actions brought, while Virginia had 59 and
> Colorado had 15. . . .
> Even in New York, Virginia, and Colorado, which reflect
> the greatest activity in this area, only a very small percentage
> of the cases were directed at actions in concert or other restric-
> tive practices designed to affect competition adversely. The
> largest number of cases listed in this category dealt with unfair
> advertising. . . . The clear evidence that insurance departments
> are unaware or seldom act in this area is found, in part, in the
> deficient examination procedures. *Data which would reveal
> anticompetitive behavior are not sought as a regular part of the
> examination procedures.*[28] [Emphasis added.]

The Limited Scope of Federal Insurance Regulation. For a period of seventy-five years prior to 1944, the federal government had little to do with the regulation of insurance. The courts had held that the business of insurance was not "commerce" within the meaning of the Constitution. Then *United States v. South-Eastern Underwriters Assn.*[29] reversed this position and the industry became subject to the Sherman, Clayton, and Federal Trade Commission Acts, with their prohibitions against restrictive, competitive, and deceptive practices.

But, as earlier noted, the effects of *South-Eastern Underwriters* were quickly overridden by the adoption of the McCarran-Ferguson Act.[30] Sections 1 and 2 of the act made it clear that the power of reg-

---

[27] *Insurance Industry Report* at 238.
[28] *Id.* at 239.
[29] 322 U.S. 533 (1944).
[30] *Supra* note 6.

ulation and taxation of the insurance industry shall continue to reside with the several states. Two exceptions, however, were grafted on the waiver of federal prerogative. First, to the extent the states do not regulate, federal law is applicable. Second, even if the states do legislate, the Sherman Act continues to strike at any "agreement to boycott, coerce, or intimidate, or act of boycott, coercion, or intimidation."

The exceptions permitting federal intervention have been read broadly by the courts. Perhaps the inadequacy of state control, coupled with the quasi-public nature of insurance, compelled an expanded reading by the judiciary. The result has been the reimposition of limited federal control in the area where the states have done so little, namely, restrictive, competitive and deceptive practices.

Thus, the Supreme Court rejected what the insurance industry seemed to have so long accepted: the ability of an insurance company's home state to control the extraterritorial activity of that company. At issue was the growing problem of mail-order insurance. Travelers Health Association, with offices in Nebraska, solicited insurance primarily through the mails. Who could impose a check on claims made by Travelers? In this instance the Federal Trade Commission, with its power to prohibit unfair or deceptive acts or practices, was allowed to intervene.[31] Using the decision as a foundation, the Federal Trade Commission, on May 5, 1964, promulgated Advertising Guides for the Mail Order Insurance Industry.[32] They are applicable to "those insurers who sell or offer to sell insurance of any kind by means of mail in any State in which they are not licensed to conduct the business of insurance, or in which, though licensed, they do not have any agents."

Similarly, the lower courts have taken the boycott exception and expanded upon it. Typically, the kind of boycott that is condemned per se under section 1 of the Sherman Act (which forbids agreements "in restraint of trade") is a *concerted refusal to deal with another*.[33] Neither joint action characterized as "peaceful persuasion"[34] nor the common imposition of something less than an

---

[31] Federal Trade Commission v. Travelers Health Assn., 362 U.S. 293 (1960).

[32] Federal Trade Commission News Release, May 5, 1964, at p. 4.

[33] Fashion Originators' Guild v. Federal Trade Commission, 312 U.S. 457 (1941).

[34] Professional and Businessmen's Life Insurance Co. v. Bankers Life Company, 163 F. Supp. 274 (D. Mont. 1958).

absolute refusal to deal[35] were sufficient to provide an escape for the insurance company defendants. What is more, the Second Circuit firmly maintained the right of private action for wrong done under the antitrust laws, including the recovery of treble damages.[36]

Perhaps the most significant development as yet applied to restrictive practices in the insurance industry has been the Antitrust Division's merger attack on Chicago Title and Trust Company. Acting under section 7 of the Clayton act, this arm of the Department of Justice has sought divestiture by Chicago Title of the Kansas City Title Insurance Company. "In its answer, Chicago Title cited the McCarran Act as barring application of the Clayton Act. But, it is the government's contention that there is no applicable state merger statute and that the states are in fact powerless to effectively regulate mergers involving insurance companies with interstate operations."[37]

If the Antitrust Division is successful, a means may have been uncovered for limiting any further tendency toward concentration. Indeed, some spokesmen for the industry have even noted and deplored the lack of state antitrust sophistication and the absence, on the state level, of antitrust know-how and experienced antitrust personnel. The answer of these insurance industry spokesmen to the problem is of interest:

> As we see it, the states have no choice; they must either develop the manpower and know-how to deal with these broader assignments or the tasks must be abandoned to the Federal government. This expansion to a more widespread review of activities with antitrust implications may be brought about in several ways. Under one approach, an individual state insurance de-

[35] California League of Independent Insurance Producers v. Aetna Casualty and Surety Co., 179 F. Supp. 65 (N.D. Calif. 1959). In another insurance case involving a boycott the language of the District Court is particularly relevant: "The Exchange also argues that the reason for the restrictive laws is to protect the American agency system. But good intent is no defense under Section 1 of the [Sherman] Act except in non per se violations where unreasonable restraints are not shown. . . . Where, as here, unreasonable restraints are shown, the requisite intent is inferred from the unlawful effects." United States v. New Orleans Insurance Exchange, 148 F. Supp. 915, 921 (E.D. La. 1957).

[36] Monarch Life Insurance Co. v. Loyal Protective Life Insurance Co., 326 F.2d 841 (2d Cir. 1963).

[37] BNA Antitrust and Trade Reg. Rep., March 10, 1964, at B-2.

partment might be expanded by the addition of an antitrust division, or antitrust personnel. Under another approach, the Department may rely on the antitrust facilities and personnel of the state attorney general's office. A third approach is to integrate the antitrust activities of both the Insurance Department and the Attorney General's office. The Federal Trade Commission and the Department of Justice have shown that close cooperation is not only possible, but is likely to lead to more effective law enforcement.[38]

Even the enlightened advocates of state antitrust enforcement have oversimplified the problems facing the insurance industry. Mergers and liquidations are but specific practices, symptomatic of the difficulties that come with size. The premiums flowing to an insurance company must be invested; by itself the company does not generate profit. In an inflationary economy, neither government nor corporate bonds allow the insurer and the insured to protect the premium dollar as well as corporate stocks. If the full measure of the insurance industry's huge capital-gathering resources should be directed to the stock market, problems of corporate concentration, asset valuation, and solvency immediately arise. The point has often been made that exaggerated considerations of solvency, which had their genesis in another economic era, have too long prohibited the life insurance industry from either contributing to or benefiting from the nation's economic growth in proportion to the industry's great capacity.

More than twenty years ago the Temporary National Economic Committee in its final report recommended that life insurance companies be permitted and encouraged to invest in common stocks. Speaking for the TNEC, Mr. Pike said:

> The aggregate size of life insurance companies is such that their investment activity vitally affects the credit and financial structure of the country. The funds which companies invest are trust funds and it is not surprising that state laws regulating life insurance companies have traditionally followed a broad pattern of permitting investments in bonds and forbidding investments in common stocks. . . . [T]he life insurance companies are ex-

[38] Insurance Series at 34.

periencing great difficulty in investing their funds. The problem in this regard is threefold. The amount of money they must invest has steadily increased. The available supply of industrial bonds, on the other hand, is gradually decreasing. The interest rates to be earned on all types of debts are inadequate in many cases when measured against the earnings which the reserve requirements of the companies make necessary.

... The life insurance companies, by far our most dynamic savings institutions, are by their operation directing an increasing amount of capital away from semispeculative or what might be called in the broadest sense of the word venture enterprises. Furthermore, their investment policies actually encourage debt financing and in so doing may eventually seriously disrupt the very business foundation upon which their prime trustee securities rest. Recognizing that life insurance funds should not be recklessly invested in highly speculative securities, there does appear to be room for the long term investment of a portion of their funds in common stocks of substantial corporations with an established record of earnings. The continued flow of funds to life insurance companies which are prevented from purchasing common stocks is certain to have serious effects on the economy. Common stocks of substantial corporations with an established record of earnings are clearly as "safe" as many bonds. A liberalization of investment laws to permit life insurance companies to invest a relatively small percentage of their funds in common stocks would stimulate healthier financial structures and have a wholesome effect upon the economy. Accordingly, it is suggested that the respective states give serious consideration to liberalizing in this direction their laws governing life insurance investments.[39]

The suggestion of the TNEC has in part been accepted. The laws of many states have been liberalized to permit insurance companies to invest a small percentage of their total assets in common stocks of high quality. But the industry continues its search for new instruments to broaden the available avenues for its tremendous

[39] Sen. Doc. No. 35, "Investigation of Concentration of Economic Power," Temporary National Economic Committee, 77th Cong., 1st Sess. (1941), at 567-68.

flow of funds. The variable annuity contract is just such an instrument. Under the terms of these contracts, the "insured" makes monthly purchase payments of fixed amounts over a period of years. The proceeds, after certain deductions, are then invested. The "insured," along with other purchasers of variable annuities, is credited monthly with "units" representing his proportionate interest in an investment fund which may be segregated from other assets of the insurance company. The value of the units, of course, will fluctuate, depending upon the investment results of the fund. And, finally, during the annuity, or "pay out" period, the "insured" receives in cash the varying value of a fixed number of units in monthly payments.

This new type of "insurance," which offers no floor but a definite ceiling, was first examined by the Supreme Court in 1959 in *Securities and Exchange Commission v. Variable Annuity Life Insurance Company.*[40] In that case a company organized exclusively for the purpose of marketing variable annuities was held subject to the disclosure and protective provisions of the Securities Act of 1933. Variable annuities were held to be securities within the meaning of the act, and the company itself, therefore, was an "investment company" subject to regulation by the SEC under the Investment Company Act of 1940.

In a later case involving Prudential Insurance Company, the Third Circuit held that a variable annuity "fund" established on the books of Prudential constituted an "investment company" subject to the act, despite the fact that Prudential itself was exempt from regulation under the Investment Company Act because it is an "insurance company." Said the Court of Appeals:

> Considerations of logic and policy provide further support for our conclusion. The Investment Company Act of 1940 contains significant safeguards for the protection of those who, like the purchasers of variable annuities, invest in "securities." These safeguards, characterized by the Commission as insuring "corporate democracy," include disclosure of investment policy and operating practices, and the regulation of fees, trading practices, and changes in investment policy. . . . The mere fact that the investment program in the case at bar is under the aegis of an insurance company ought not to negate compliance

[40] 359 U.S. 65 (1959).

with these controls in the absence of compelling circumstances.[41]

Federal regulation now combines with state control in protecting the insured. But what of the power that flows to the insurance company through investments in common stocks? What dangers are presented to the shareholders of the portfolio corporations? Save for boycotts and mergers, the federal government by statute lacks the authority to intervene. And the states, whatever their laws may declare, often do not have the capacity to act.

On neither the federal nor the state level has industry regulation been viewed in a context other than protection of policyholders. It may well be that the flow of life insurance funds into the capital market has been too long confined to specific and somewhat arbitrarily restrictive forms, but it is also true that the impact of industry conduct on portfolio companies has been too long ignored. While the simple mathematical limitations on percentage ownership of equity securities may serve to foster solvency through portfolio diversification, they are a poor substitute for the development of fiduciary standards of conduct to accompany the accumulation of economic power. As the magnitude of the accumulated power and wealth of the nation grows, formulation of proper standards of responsibility for control of this wealth becomes a problem that far transcends the question of decentralization. We have reached the point where one need not be dominant to be powerful. Nowhere is this more applicable than in the life insurance industry.

To be sure, the combination of state and federal regulation is comprehensive, but it is not necessarily perfect. Life insurance must fulfill certain needs if it is to survive and continue as a useful financial institution. But the public needs of 1930 are not those of the 1960's. The premium on security and safety that may well have been worth paying in 1930 is perhaps not worth the price demanded in the 1960's, in part because the spiral of inflation has made the the price too high, and in part because the evolution of a semi-controlled economy has reduced the need for that protection. Through a truly unique combination of government and business growth, the nation's economy has reached a level of maturation

[41] Prudential Insurance Company v. Securities and Exchange Commission, 326 F. 2d 383, 388 (3d Cir. 1964).

completely different from anything known prior to 1930. Its most violent swings appear to have been curtailed. Under these circumstances the price for absolute safety is too much in terms of tomorrow's deflated dollars.

All of this is not without industry recognition. The life companies are sadly aware of their diminishing percentage of the overall savings dollar. The declining position of insured pension plans, relative to trusteed and self-administered plans, has been striking. The advantages of equity growth and increased income are by statute denied to the life companies. Obviously, the development of the variable annuity is an effort to overcome this handicap. But trusteed pension plans are far ahead. While the insurance industry continues to struggle with administrative hurdles, striving to make the variable annuity generally available, the trusteed pension funds have run away with the idea. Increasingly, corporate pension plans are offering a combination of fixed and variable benefits, and this trend will certainly increase as unions discover how much the employer can save under a fixed-benefit plan from a small increase in fund earnings. Some experts have estimated that a 1 per cent increase in pension fund yield will normally either *decrease* the employer's costs by 20 per cent or *increase* the employee's benefits by 25 per cent! Employers will not long be able to reap *all* of this benefit.

While it must be admitted that solvency and the possibilities of concentration of control are potential problems of increased equity investment by life insurance companies, they are problems that must be viewed in the light of today's facts, not in the shadow of a bygone economic era. As we have seen in other contexts, prohibition provides a clean sweep, but not necessarily the best working solution to a problem.

BANKING

Uniqueness of Banking. Commercial banks are unique among financial institutions in that they alone are permitted by law to accept demand deposits. This distinctive power gives commercial banking a key role in the national economy. For banks do not merely deal in, but are actually a source of money and credit; when a bank makes a loan by crediting the borrower's demand deposit account, it augments the Nation's credit supply. Furthermore, the power to accept demand deposits makes banks the intermediaries in most financial transactions (since transfer of substantial moneys are almost always by check rather than by cash) and, concomitantly, the repositories of very substantial individual and corporate funds.[42] While banks have traditionally been the primary suppliers of commercial credit, their need for liquidity resulting from demand deposits has generally caused them to limit their investments to short-term credit and high grade government securities.

Only in recent years have banks begun to participate with the life insurance companies in affording long-term (over one year) credit that is not secured by a mortgage of specific physical assets. And even more recently have some banks become major suppliers of consumer installment loans which are not only essential to mass distribution of products, but have also become an important segment of corporate borrowing. Banking over the years has grown tremendously in size as well as in the scope of its activities. Today commercial banking describes a wide variety of services and credit devices which include unsecured personal and business loans, mortgage loans, loans secured by securities or accounts receivable, consumer goods installment loans, tuition financing, bank credit cards, revolving credit funds, acceptance of demand deposits from individuals, corporations, governmental agencies, and other banks, acceptance of time and savings deposits, estate and trust planning and trusteeship services, lock boxes and safety-deposit boxes, account reconciliation services, foreign department services (acceptances and letters of credit), correspondent services and investment advice. Of course, other institutions are in the business of supplying credit and thus are more or less in competition with commercial banks. For example, mutual savings banks, savings and loan associations, credit unions, personal-finance companies, sales-finance companies, private businessmen (through the furnishing of trade credit), factors, direct-lending government agencies, the Post Office, small business investment companies, and life insurance companies all compete directly or indirectly with commercial banks.

The Nature of Banking Regulation. Banking, even more than insurance, is subject to an intricate web of federal and state regulation. Banks are specially chartered under state statutes or

---

[42] United States v. Philadelphia National Bank, 374 U.S. 321, 326 (1963).

as national banks under the National Banking Act. The flow of funds to and from commercial banks is measured by the Comptroller of the Currency and, in the case of banks affiliated with the Federal Reserve System, by the Board of Governors of that organization as well. In addition, the vast majority of all banks are insured by the Federal Deposit Insurance Corporation and thus must meet the regulatory standards of that agency. But despite the complexity and diversity of regulation, banks have retained an economic role that makes them something short of a "public utility." James J. Saxon, Comptroller of the Currency, has noted this distinction:

> The banks of our country are not . . . controlled in the same degree as the "public utilities." This difference is of vital significance in determining the proper role of competition in the field of banking. In the public utility industries, the cost conditions which prevail require in many instances the granting of monopoly powers as a means of assuring service and avoiding destructive competition. Accordingly, in that industry, in addition to the regulation of entry, the serving of public convenience and need is made mandatory, and the terms under which those services are offered are publicly controlled. Neither of these latter two forms of public control is applied to the field of banking. . . . In banking, even though entry is regulated, there is broad scope for the exercise of private initiative. Unfortunately, the significance of this distinction is not always fully understood.[43]

The key object of banking regulation is, of course, solvency, the protection of depositors' funds.

> If a bank fails and if there is no insurance for the depositor, then the depositor can lose all. Experience has shown that competition will inadequately guard the public against the danger, since when a bank fails it is too late for the depositors to take their business elsewhere . . . While competition will weed out those who cut too many corners, the public can be badly hurt in the process. The reasons normally given for preventing

[43] Address by James J. Saxon, "Competition in Banking," at the 69th Annual Convention of the Kentucky Bankers Association, Louisville, Kentucky, Oct. 22, 1962, at pp. 2-3.

banks from paying interest on demand deposits, or from paying more than a prescribed maximum on savings deposits, or from allowing free entry, or for controlling their portfolios are based on the argument that banks must be kept sound.[44]

Solvency, while most important, is not the only object of banking controls; regulation is necessary to insure liquidity, to encourage competition and thus foster the development of a wide range of banking services at the lowest possible cost. More recently banks, as well as stock insurance companies, have become subject to regulations designed to protect their shareholders, similar to the reporting, proxy-soliciting, and insider-trading rules that have long applied to commercial and industrial companies whose stocks are listed on a securities exchange. Prior to adoption of the Securities Acts Amendments of 1964, these long-accepted safeguards for shareholders of industrial companies were not available to bank or insurance company shareholders, who were often hard put to find out even the barest facts about their investments.

With the exception of the usury laws of the several states, the forces of competition are relied upon to achieve low bank charges. Administrative edict enters only to insure that competition, not combination, is the guide to a bank's operations. Yet, to the extent that concentration permeates the industry, to the extent that the entrance of new banks is rendered unlikely under the guise of assuring solvency, how great a role can competition play? Professor Donald Dewey observed:

> [W]here . . . power to exclude newcomers is present—competition will most probably degenerate into some form of oligopoly. One may, for example, safely predict that any town which limits the number of taxicab permits while allowing them to be bought and sold in a free market will shortly witness a rapid consolidation of firms.[45]

Through the banks there originates and flows much of the nation's money supply. The Federal Reserve Board, through its

---

[44] Moore, *The Philadelphia-Girard Decision—Some Further Comments,* 1 THE NATIONAL BANKING REVIEW 407, 413 (1964).

[45] DEWEY, MONOPOLY IN ECONOMICS AND LAW 26 (1959).

control over the rediscount rates, has enormous power to constrict or expand bank reserves with the anticipated result that availability and cost of business and consumer credit will accordingly be affected in the desired manner. Yet, it must be noted, a bank that holds a monopoly may feel slight compulsion to respond to Federal Reserve decision.

[I]t may consider its profits sufficient. If there is considerable competition, however, an institution will either respond quickly and actively seek out markets for funds or find itself falling behind in the race with shrinking deposits and profits. Again it would seem that competition serves the public interest, notwithstanding the presence of regulations. It is more than coincidental that, in small towns with only one or two banks, changes in interest charges and lending policies are infrequent.[46]

At least insofar as solvency is concerned, the goals of banking regulation seem to be relatively well met. For the entire country there were but three bank suspensions in 1957, two in 1960, and nine in 1961. How sharply this contrasts with the six hundred bank failures for a single year in the 1920's. This dramatic change has largely been the result of the complex of banking rules, mostly adopted during the depression, governing entry, branching, and acquisitions.

A charter for a new bank, state or national, will not be granted unless the invested capital and management of the applicant, and its prospects for doing sufficient business to operate at a reasonable profit, give adequate protection against undue competition and possible failure.[47] Failure to meet these standards may cause the Federal Deposit Insurance Corporation (FDIC) to refuse an application for insurance,[48] and may cause the FDIC, the Federal Reserve Board, or the Comptroller to refuse permission to branch to insured, member, or national banks, respectively.[49] Permission to merge, consolidate, acquire

---

[46] *Supra* note 44, at 414-15: 12 U.S.C. §§ 462, 462b; see also 12 U.S.C. §§ 263(c), 353-59 with respect to control over the rediscount rate.

[47] 12 U.S.C. §§ 26, 27, 51.

[48] 12 U.S.C. §§ 1815, 1816.

[49] 12 U.S.C. §§ 36, 321, 1828(d).

assets, or assume liabilities may be refused by the agencies on the same grounds.[50] Furthermore, national banks appear to be subject to state geographical limitations on branching.[51] Banks are also subject to a number of specific provisions aimed at ensuring sound banking practices. For example, member banks of the Federal Reserve System may not pay interest on demand deposits . . . or hold for their own accounts securities of any one obligor in excess of 10% of the bank's unimpaired capital and surplus . . . and may not pay interest on time or savings deposits above the rate fixed by the Federal Reserve Board. The payment of interest on deposits by nonmember insured banks is also federally regulated. . . .

But perhaps the most effective weapon of federal regulation of banking is the broad visitorial power of federal bank examiners. . . . [S]hould they discover unsound banking practices, they are equipped with a formidable array of sanctions . . . [that include termination by the FDIC of] the bank's insured status.[52]

Concentration—The Banking Oligopoly. The primacy of solvency in the scheme of things has had a marked effect on the industry and the regulators. The barriers against entry appear to have stimulated a push toward concentration.[53] From 1953 to 1962 there was a net decline of 647 in the number of banks. During this period approximately 175 banks went out of existence each year. About 95 per cent of these merged with other banks; and 17 in 20 of this total continued as branches of the surviving banks.

Newly organized banks—a total of 1113—only partially offset the number of discontinued—1760. Over this period, however, the rate of decline in the number of banks lessened steadily, from a net loss of more than 100 banks per year in 1953-54 to only about 25 banks per year in 1961-62.

The slower rate of decline reflects primarily a doubling in the number of new banks organized. . . .

[50] 12 U.S.C. § 1828(c).
[51] 12 U.S.C. § 36(c).
[52] *Supra* note 42 at 329-30.
[53] Celler, *The Philadelphia National Bank Case—A Rejoinder,* 1 NATIONAL BANKING REVIEW 229 (1963).

For the country as a whole, these changes in the banking structure have been accomplished by little change in the concentration of deposits held by a given number or percentage of the largest banks. For example, the 100 largest banks at the end of 1962 held about 48 percent of total deposits, only a little more than 10 years earlier and much less than the 58 percent they held in 1940.[54]

James J. Saxon, Comptroller of the Currency, has taken issue with the charge of undue limitations on entrance into banking:

During the past year we experienced a strong upsurge of interest by new sources of capital and enterprise desirous of entering the field of banking. Well-capitalized, competent groups have been formed in many parts of the country to seek new bank charters. Chiefly, the new applications have come from the States which impose severe restrictions over bank expansion.

Of the 149 applications for new National Bank charters received last year, 98 were from 13 of the States which prohibit branch banking, 35 of the applications were from Florida, 26 from Texas, 9 from Colorado, 5 from Illinois, and 4 from Wisconsin—all no-branch States. The present breadth of interest in the field of banking is indicated by the fact that 37 States were represented in last year's list of new National Bank charter applications. These applications in 1962 were nearly triple the average annual applications for the preceding decade, and approximately double the highest year during that period. For the preceding decade, applications for new National Bank charters were as low as 39 in 1952, and ranged between 71 and 75 in the years 1955, 1959, 1960, and 1961.[55]

The importance of these statistics lies in the fact that where concentration gives rise to oligopoly, competition among the oligopolists can play but a minimal role. And, as we shall see, oligopoly does in fact characterize the banking industry. Practically speaking, oligopoly for banking means the lack of competition *within* the

[54] *Changes in Banking Structure,* 49 FED. RESERVE BULL. 1191, 1193-94 (1963).
[55] Saxon, *Banking Expansion and Economic Growth—A New Perspective,* 8 ANTITRUST BULL. 597, 602-03 (1963).

industry, but does not preclude an aggressive response to the challenges of other industries. To illustrate, consider the recently concluded antitrust consent decrees against a number of Minnesota banks. Each of the defendants under the terms of the decrees was prohibited from agreeing to fix the rate of interest on loans, from limiting the solicitation of business by any bank, or from preventing the absorption of exchange charges or losses on securities for any third person.[56] In still another consent decree, entered in 1962, several New Jersey banks were forbidden from combining to set checking service charges.[57]

Recognizing the day-to-day supervision of the bank supervisory agencies, the interesting questions are how such cases arose in the first instance, and why it took the "nonexpert" Antitrust Division to prosecute them. Professor Herman of the Wharton School of Finance and Commerce reasoned:

> The bank supervisory authorities are in continuous contact with the bankers under their jurisdiction, and policymakers among the supervisory authorities tend to be drawn from among the bankers themselves. Since bankers are deeply concerned with supervisory policies, they inevitably exercise their political influence to assure the selection of sympathetic authorities. Continuous contact and interaction tend to consolidate what frequently amounts to a tacit alliance. The regulators do not merely regulate; they represent and lead the regulated.[58]

Indeed, only after the Antitrust Division prosecuted under the Sherman Act did the Comptroller of the Currency feel obliged to adopt regulations prohibiting agreements to fix service charges. Yet even here the warm-tempered hand of the Comptroller can be

---

[56] United States v. Northwestern National Bank, Trade Reg. Rep., 1964 Trade Cas., ¶71,020 (D. Minn. March 24, 1964); United States v. The First National Bank of Saint Paul, Trade Reg. Rep., 1964 Trade Cas., ¶71,021 (D. Minn. March 24, 1964); United States v. Duluth Clearing House Assn., Trade Reg. Rep., 1964 Trade Cas., ¶71,022 (D. Minn. March 24, 1964).

[57] United States v. Hunterdon County Trust Co., Trade Reg. Rep., 1962 Trade Cas., ¶70,263 (D. N.J. April 16, 1962).

[58] Herman, *The Philadelphia Bank Decision and its Critics,* 1 THE NATIONAL BANKING REVIEW 391, 404-05 (1964).

observed. The summary and comment on the new rules by the Comptroller's counsel states:

> *Although it was recognized that identical charges for identical services may occur even in the absence of any agreement . . . among banks . . .* National Banks *were cautioned* that each must be prepared to demonstrate conclusively to the Comptroller that its scale of service charges was adopted unilaterally, and not on the basis of any agreement or understanding, or even discussion, among banks or their officers.[59] [Emphasis added.]

On the scale of values of the regulators, competition among the regulated apparently does not weigh heavily. For the Office of Comptroller, the facts are damning. From 1950 to May 1, 1955, the Comptroller approved 376 consecutive bank mergers and consolidations, without a single intervening disapproval. And what is more significant, he failed to specify to the national bank examiners initially reviewing merger petitions the import of competition in proposed bank mergers.

The 14,399 commercial banks in 1940 dwindled to 14,164 by 1950, 13,472 by 1960, and 13,429 by 1962. Representative Celler, an architect of recent antitrust legislation, recalled the facts of concentration:

> I pointed out, in 1959, that in ten of the nation's sixteen leading financial centers, four banks owned more than 80 percent of all commercial assets. . . . [I]n nine of these financial centers, two banks owned more than 60 percent of all commercial assets. . . . [I]n each of sixteen financial centers, the first four banks owned 60 percent of all the commercial assets; and the first two banks, more than 40 percent.[60]

Viewing the United States as a whole does not detract from the sampling by Representative Celler. Using statistics compiled by the Federal Deposit Insurance Corporation, these findings emerge for

[59] *Current Legal and Regulatory Developments,* 1 THE NATIONAL BANKING REVIEW 133, 137-38 (1963). "Each bank was directed to review and reestablish its scale of service charges independent of any relationship with any other bank —such revised scale to be made in accordance with what is deemed necessary or *desirable* in the light of the individual bank's cost and competitive position."

[60] *Supra* note 53, at 232.

the year 1962: The largest hundred commercial banks and bank groups controlled 49.4 per cent of all deposits. The largest ten held 21.8 per cent; the largest five, 14.6 per cent; the largest three, 10.5 per cent; and the largest bank, 4.4 per cent.[61]

Undoubtedly, the strongest force contributing to banking concentration in recent years has been the accelerating rate of mergers. From 1950 to 1960 more than sixteen hundred banks with resources in excess of $33 billion were absorbed by merger. The facts were thus described by Representative Celler:

> Between 1953 and 1962, there were 1,669 mergers and absorptions of commercial banks and 1,113 new banks organized. States in which statewide branching is prevalent had a net loss of 330 banks in the ten-year period, a 25 percent decline. Because of mergers, more than one in every three banks existing in 1952 was eliminated as a separate institution; and only 166 new banks were organized.[62]

While economists may argue the scope of concentration, Congress assessed its reality in the banking industry and, as a result, adopted the Bank Merger Act of 1960.[63] Under this statute, the respective agencies were ordered to consider the competitive impact of all proposed mergers of banks within their jurisdiction. The statute provides that, in granting or withholding consent, the bank regulatory agencies shall consider the financial history and condition of each of the banks involved, the adequacy of its capital structure, its future earnings prospects, the general character of its management, and the convenience and needs of the community to be served. The appropriate agency is also required to consider the effect of the transaction on competition (including any tendency toward monopoly), and not approve the transaction unless, after considering all of such factors, it finds that the transaction is in the public interest.

But for all of Congress' concern, the federal agencies charged with administering the Bank Merger Act seemed to show slight regard for the element of competition.

---

[61] 1962 FDIC ANN. REP. 53.

[62] *Supra* note 53, at 232-33.

[63] 12 U.S.C. § 1828(c) (1963 ed. Supp. IV).

In 1961 the Comtroller of the Currency approved 69 merger applications and denied two; in 1962 he approved 110 and denied seven. Between 1962 and June 30, 1963, he approved 35 and denied one. The Federal Reserve Board's record for the same periods was 32 approved, five denied; 37 approved, five denied; and 18 approved, one denied. The record for the Federal Deposit Insurance Corporation was 31 approved, none denied; 44 approved, none denied respectively, and 14 approved, none denied. The record for prior years is even more uniform in result. It may be that most of these merger applications merited approval, but the record is so one-sided as to raise some doubts as to a system which leads to such results.[64]

It should not have been a surprise, therefore, when the Justice Department's Antitrust Division sought to apply section 7 of the Clayton Act in an effort to obtain some judicial restraints on proposed bank mergers.[65] Section 7, briefly stated, prohibits all asset or stock acquisitions which may substantially lessen competition. The first bank merger litigated by the Antitrust Division was that of the Philadelphia National Bank (PNB) and Girard Trust Corn Exchange Bank (Girard), the second and third largest of the forty-two commercial banks with headquarters in the Philadelphia metropolitan area.[66] As of 1959 PNB had assets in excess of $1 billion, and Girard, $750 million. Noting that both banks attained their size in part through mergers the Court assessed the power that would attach to the proposed single entity. The resulting bank would have been the largest in the Philadelphia area with 36 per cent of the area banks' total assets, 36 per cent of deposits, and 34 per cent of net loans.

The facts before the Court did not discourage it from finding that the Bank Merger Act *allowed*, rather than precluded, application of section 7 of the Clayton Act to the banking industry. Said the Court:

> Nor did Congress, in passing the Bank Merger Act, embrace the view that federal regulation of banking is so comprehensive

---

[64] *Supra* note 53, at 235-36.
[65] 15 U.S.C. § 18.
[66] United States v. Philadelphia National Bank, 374 U.S. 321 (1963).

that enforcement of the antitrust laws would be either unnecessary, in light of the completeness of the regulatory structure, or disruptive of that structure. On the contrary, the legislative history of the [Bank Merger] Act seems clearly to refute any suggestion that applicability of the antitrust laws was to be affected. . . . Moreover, bank regulation is in most respects less complete than public utility regulation, to which interstate rail and air carriers, among others, are subject. Rate regulation in the banking industry is limited and largely indirect . . . ; banks are under no duty not to discriminate in their services; and though the location of bank offices is regulated, banks may do business—place loans and solicit deposits—where they please. The fact that the banking agencies maintain a close surveillance of the industry with a view toward preventing unsound practices that might impair liquidity or lead to insolvency does not make federal banking regulation all-pervasive, although it does minimize the hazards of intense competition. Indeed, that there are so many direct public controls over unsound competitive practices in the industry refutes the argument that private controls of competition are necessary in the public interest and ought therefore to be immune from scrutiny under the antitrust laws.[67]

Repeating the rationale that led to its condemnation of the merger, the Court stated:

There is no reason to think that concentration is less inimical to the free play of competition in banking than in other service industries. On the contrary, it is in all probability more inimical. For example banks compete to fill the credit needs of businessmen. Small businessmen especially are, as a practical matter, confined to their locality for the satisfaction of their credit needs. If the number of banks in the locality is reduced, the vigor of competition for filling the marginal small business borrower's needs is likely to diminish. At the same time, his concomitantly greater difficulty in obtaining credit is likely to put him at a disadvantage *vis-à-vis* larger businesses with which

[67] *Id.* at 352.

he competes. In this fashion, concentration in banking accelerates concentration generally.[68]

The Antitrust Division's attack on bank mergers did not rest solely on the Clayton Act. The Division in another case[69] also cited the Sherman Act and what many once considered a discarded theory, namely, that any merger involving substantial competitors is a combination in restraint of trade. Or, putting it more simply, "bigness," in this context, is bad.

The facts again provided both the foundation and the impetus for the Court's ruling. Despite negative reports from three agencies, the FDIC, the Federal Reserve, and the Attorney General, the Comptroller approved a proposed merger between the first- and fourth-largest banks in Lexington, Kentucky. The largest bank held 39 per cent of the area banks' assets, 40 per cent of deposits, and 40 per cent of loans. The fourth-ranking bank held 12.8 per cent of assets, 11.8 per cent of deposits, and 13.9 per cent of loans.

Was the acquisition a combination in restraint of trade? The Court had to face and distinguish the oft-cited *Columbia Steel*[70] decision, to which students and practitioners refer when they claim that "bigness" alone is not bad. There the Court approved the asset acquisition of Consolidated Steel Corporation by United States Steel Corporation. While the same weight was given to the inability of United States Steel to compete with Consolidated because of rate structure and location, the Court defined these guides for measuring legality:

> In determining what constitutes unreasonable restraint, we do not think the dollar volume is in itself of compelling significance; we look rather to the percentage of business controlled, the strength of the remaining competition, whether the action springs from business requirements or purpose to monopolize, the probable development of the industry, consumer demands, and other characteristics of the market. We do not undertake to prescribe any set of percentage figures by

[68] *Id.* at 369-70.
[69] United States v. First National Bank & Trust Company of Lexington, 376 U.S. 665 (1964).
[70] United States v. Columbia Steel Co., 334 U.S. 495 (1948).

which to measure the reasonableness of a corporation's en-
largement of its activities by the purchase of the assets of a
competitor. The relative effect of percentage command of a
market varies with the setting in which that factor is placed.[71]

Fully quoting this excerpt, the Court in the *Lexington* case
summarily concluded: "In the present case all those factors [ed.
of *Columbia Steel*] point the other way. . . . Where, as here, the
merging companies are major competitive factors in a relevant
market, the elimination of significant competition between them
constitutes a violation of § 1 of the Sherman Act."[72] Like it or
not, *Columbia Steel* has undergone extensive judicial surgery. For
purposes of mergers at least, bigness in many respects can be
considered bad, especially where the merging entities serve the
same "relevant market."

What, then, is the import of these two recent Supreme Court
decisions? On the positive side, a means finally may have been
found to *arrest* further concentration in the banking industry.
But, apparently, that is all. These salutory cases come on the heels
of a long succession of mergers among New York City banks, involving and resulting in some of the largest banks in the country.
It seems highly unlikely that either the Sherman or Clayton Act
can or will be used to disintegrate the oligopoly that already exists
in the banking industry. Concentration in banking *is* and will
remain a fact of life.

From the Supreme Court decisions comes one final thought.
The banking regulatory agencies apparently have either little understanding or minimal motivation to foster competition. By this we
do not mean to cast doubts on the integrity of any agency. We
mean only to say that where the first concern of the regulators so
long has been solvency, they, like the industry, seem to under-
estimate the importance of all other factors, including the importance of competition in a free society.

Trust Control and Power. A major source of a bank's strength
as a financial intermediary lies in its trust department. Where
the trust instrument permits discretionary investments and the
right to vote stock held for the beneficiaries (as is commonly the

[71] *Id.* at 527-28.
[72] *Supra* note 69, at 672-73.

case), a bank is given enormous powers that could be employed to check the managements of its portfolio corporations. It is in this area that the Comptroller of the Currency may require a national bank's fidelity as trustee for its beneficiaries.

Until 1962 the control of national bank trust operations rested with the Board of Governors of the Federal Reserve System. Legislation was then passed to vest such supervision in the Comptroller of the Currency.[73] The Comptroller's regulations provide insight into the kind of control exercised, as well as the power of a bank's trust department:[74]

(1) Where an agency agreement bestows upon the bank the power of attorney and investment discretion, monies may now be invested in a common trust fund; heretofore banks have had to invest such funds separately.

(2) Similarly, qualified pension plans may be lumped together for purposes of collective investment.

(3) No longer is the $100,000 limit on a single participation in a common trust fund applicable. Now a single participant may hold up to 10% of the common fund, and, in addition, 10% of the fund may be invested in a single security.

(4) A national bank may sell assets held by it as fiduciary in one account to itself as fiduciary in another account if the transaction is fair to both accounts and if such transaction is not prohibited by the terms of any governing instrument or by local law.

(5) A national bank may make a loan to an account from the funds belonging to another such account, when the making of such loans to a designated account is authorized by the instrument creating the account from which such loans are made, and is not prohibited by local law.

(6) A national bank may make a loan to an account and may take as security therefore assets of the account, provided such transaction is fair to such account and is not prohibited by local law.

The effect of these regulations is to give the national banks the

[73] 12 U.S.C. § 92(a).
[74] 12 C.F.R. § 9.12 *et seq.*

greatest possible flexibility in their competition for trust business. Funds may be commingled to provide more elasticity in investment. Toward this end, both the restrictions of common law fiduciary concepts and the danger of portfolio concentration are partially overlooked. Perhaps the Supreme Court was aware of these facts when, for the first time, it called attention to the trust powers that would exist if two powerful banks in Lexington, Kentucky, had been permitted to remain merged: "Prior to the consolidation, First National and Security Trust had been close competitors in the trust department business. Between them they held 94.82% of all trust assets, 92.20% of all trust department earnings, and 79.62% of all trust accounts."[75]

Like other aspects of the banking industry, concentration also characterizes the trust business, which represents "one of the main fiduciary groups in the country."[76] Further, a portion of those trusts administered are combined individual funds, a factor that removes the trustee from the direct control of any one person. Among the consequences flowing from this is to heighten the power position of banks in relation to portfolio corporations, for the monies coming into the trust departments are plentiful and may be directed, subject to some limitations, as the department desires.

There is yet another consequence springing from merging and concentrating trust business, and that is the danger of conflicts of interest.[77] A single trust department, charged with administering a large number of accounts and frequently vested with wide discretionary powers, may find it difficult to remain entirely faithful to all of them. Within the framework of national banking regulation, efforts are made to achieve this end. Responsibility for the proper exercise of fiduciary duties is placed squarely and exclusively with a bank's board of directors. Regular audits are required. Moreover the quality and nature of investments made are the proper subject of examination by the Comptroller. And, finally, each collective investment fund must be founded and maintained on the basis of a plan approved by a bank's board of directors and filed with the Comptroller.

[75] *Supra* note 69, at 669.
[76] Statement of William McC. Martin, Chairman, Board of Governors of the Federal Reserve System, before the House Committee on Banking and Currency, Sept. 24, 1963, reprinted in 49 FED. RESERVE BULL., 1370, 1375 (1963).
[77] *Id.* at 1377.

The Plan shall contain appropriate provisions not inconsistent with the rules and regulations of the Comptroller of the Currency as to the manner in which the fund is to be operated, including provisions relating to the investment powers of the bank with respect to the fund, the allocation of income, profits and losses, the terms and conditions governing the admission or withdrawal of participations in the fund, the auditing of accounts of the bank with respect to the fund, the basis and method of valuing assets in the fund, the minimum frequency for valuation of assets of the fund, the period following each such valuation date during which the valuation may be made, the basis upon which the fund may be terminated, and such other matters as may be necessary to define clearly the rights of participants in the fund.[78]

Again, however, we see control directed toward the goal of solvency, toward the faithful, efficient administration of trusts. These are worthy objectives, to be sure, but there appears to be room for little else. Concentration, restrictive practices, and the steady lessening of competition evidently are not a serious concern of the Comptroller.

INVESTMENT COMPANIES

In sharp contrast to the maze of multiple-agency federal and state regulations affecting banks, the regulation of investment companies is largely covered by the Investment Company Act of 1940, administered by the Securities and Exchange Commission. (This is so even though investment companies, like other corporations, are affected by the corporate laws of the state of incorporation and, of course, by special provisions of the Internal Revenue Code allowing them to pass through tax-free income to their stockholders.) The 1940 act leaves no question about the evils Congress sought to eliminate in adopting the most comprehensive of all the federal securities laws. It states that "the national public interest and the interest of investors are adversely affected" by the following circumstances: (1) when investors do not receive adequate, accurate, and explicit information, fairly presented, concerning the character of their securities and the circumstances, policies, and

[78] 12 C.F.R. § 917 *et seq.* (Jan. 1, 1964).

financial responsibility of the companies and their management, (2) when investment companies are managed in the interest of their directors, officers, or other special-interest groups rather than in the interest of all classes of such companies' security holders, (3) when investment companies issue securities containing inequitable or discriminatory provisions, or fail to protect the preferences and privileges of the holders of their outstanding securities, (4) when investment company control is unduly concentrated through such methods as pyramiding, or when they are managed by irresponsible persons, (5) when investment companies employ unsound methods of account, or are not subjected to adequate independent scrutiny, (6) when fundamental corporate changes are made without the consent of the investment company shareholders, (7) when excessive borrowing increases unduly the speculative character of the investment companies' junior securities, (8) when investment companies operate without adequate assets or reserves.[79] These practices were condemned as a result of an exhaustive study by the SEC of investment trusts and companies, which culminated in the adoption of the 1940 statute.

The Investment Company Act is easily the most complex of the six major statutes that the SEC administers. Its philosophy represents a marked departure from the underlying principle of disclosure, which is the basic tenet of the Securities Act of 1933 and the Securities Exchange Act of 1934. The Investment Company Act is *regulatory;* in this instance, mere disclosure would not suffice to remedy the wrongs found in the investment company industry. Thus, investment companies are subject to controls requiring registration with, and reporting to, the SEC; newly organized companies must have an initial net worth of $100,000; certain persons are ineligible to serve as officers, directors, or investment advisers of investment companies; margin accounts, joint trading accounts, short sales, dealings with affiliated persons, corporate pyramiding, and interlocks with insurance companies are all prohibited; fundamental investment policies may not be changed without shareholder approval; diversified companies may not concentrate their holdings in a single issue in excess of a specified

---

[79] Investment Company Act of 1940, Section 1(b), 15 U.S.C. § 80a-1(b) (1958).

percentage, and investment advisory and underwriting contracts must be approved at least annually by the shareholders or a disinterested majority of directors. Moreover, the capital structure of investment companies must meet specified requirements and the board of directors must be composed of at least 40 per cent "outside" directors.[80]

An additional sanction is provided by section 36, which gives the Commission the right to seek the removal of any investment company officer or director for any "gross misconduct or gross abuse of trust." Unlike a similar provision of New York law, section 36 is not a dead letter. *Aldred Investment Trust v. Securities and Exchange Commission*[81] is proof of this. Aldred could not meet the interest requirements for $5.9 million of debentures held by the public. The SEC vetoed plans for reorganization proposed by the company, for in every case the plan called for a sacrifice of the rights of the debenture holders. The principal stockholder rejected the Commission's suggestion for liquidating part of the company's portfolio. The portfolio, he said, consisted of high-grade utilities that were yielding an excellent return but were underpriced on the market.

Then, with inadequate notice to those who had a stake in the company, the principal stockholder caused the company to exercise an option for the purchase of the controlling interest in a race track. The price paid by the investment company for the race track stock was $80 a share; the market price ranged from $52 to $59 for small blocks of stock. The difference represented "a premium for control." To raise the necessary cash, the trust was forced to liquidate 30 per cent of its portfolio. Among the securities sold were those Hanlon, the principal stockholder, had told the SEC should not be sold hastily or in large blocks. In addition, some of the trust's securities were apparently sold at prices under the market. On coming to power the investment company trustees "promptly elected themselves directors" of the race track at salaries as high as $25,000 a year, although they apparently had no knowledge of how to manage such a business.

In affirming the district court's finding of a "gross abuse of

[80] 15 U.S.C. § 80a-6 *et seq.*
[81] 151 F.2d 254 (1st Cir. 1944), *cert. denied*, 326 U.S. 795 (1946).

trust" under section 36, the appellate court ignored the exculpatory clauses which girded the investment company and allowed the appointment of receivers. The court stated:

> [T]he only effective means of protecting the interests of the debenture holders was to remove Hanlon from the control of the trust assets which do not belong to him. Section 36 invokes the equity power of the Federal Court that calls into play its inherent powers to do justice and grant full relief. The appointment of receivers in the case at bar was an appropriate exercise of the court's inherent equity power.[82]

In support of its decision the court cited with approval *Pepper v. Litton:*

> He who is in such a fiduciary position cannot serve himself first and his *cestuis* second. . . . He cannot use his power for his personal advantage and to the detriment of the stockholders and creditors no matter how absolute in terms that power may be and no matter how meticulous he is to satisfy technical requirements. For that power is at all times subject to the equitable limitation that it may not be exercised for the aggrandizement, preference, or advantage of the fiduciary to the exclusion or detriment of the *cestuis*. Where there is a violation of those principles, equity will undo the wrong or intervene to prevent its consummation.[83]

To the SEC the *Aldred* case tended to confirm their belief that "the terms 'misconduct' and 'abuse of trust' contained in Section 36, while not excluding violations of statutory provisions, thus have a wider significance." The Commission, however, was not successful in extending this position in *Securities and Exchange Commission v. Insurance Securities, Inc.*[84] Under attack in this case was the sale of the controlling stock interest of the fund's investment adviser and principal underwriter at a price twenty-five times in excess of the adviser's book value. The fund was controlled by the directors of the adviser. It was the contention of the SEC that "the

---

[82] *Id.* at 260.
[83] 308 U.S. 295 (1939).
[84] 254 F.2d 642 (9th Cir. 1958).

excess" represented "payment for succession to the adviser's or underwriter's fiduciary office and undertaking." The Commission's position was not based on any claim that the adviser's stock had been sold to irresponsible persons, but rather, pointing to the familiar cases of *Clarke v. Greenberg*,[85] *Gerdes v. Reynolds*,[86] and *Perlman v. Feldmann*,[87] the Commission contended that the directors of the adviser had breached their fiduciary duty by selling what by analogy amounted to a corporate office of the fund. The court rejected this view. Section 15(a)(4) of the Investment Company Act of 1940 provides for the automatic termination of service contracts when the investment adviser transfers control to another. Further, the court held that no corporate opportunity had been appropriated. While it recognized that the price paid for the adviser's stock was based primarily on the prospect that the service contracts with the fund would be renewed and the profits thus would continue to be received, the court stated: "This prospect no more represents an asset of Trust Fund than do the current profits to the service company, as received. The price received by appellee-directors for their stock in the service company did not come from the coffers of the investment company, but from outside purchasers."[88]

One commentator on the *Insurance Securities* decision noted:

[T]he price did reflect the purchasers' confidence that through control of the proxy machinery there would be a renewal of the contract and thus a succession to the fiduciary office. Moreover, even if theoretically there could be no transfer, there may be a breach of fiduciary duty in the acceptance of a price based on contract expectancy. . . . The basis of the rule that a fiduciary cannot accept compensation for a transfer of his office is not that he thereby transfers an asset, but rather that he cannot exploit his position for personal profit because of the danger of conflicting interests. Even under the court's analysis, the proxy machinery might be regarded as an asset of the Fund and some of the consideration might be allocated to

[85] 71 N.E.2d 443 (N.Y. 1947).
[86] 28 N.Y.S.2d 622 (1941).
[87] 129 F. Supp. 162 (D. Conn. 1952), *rev'd*, 219 F.2d 173 (2d Cir. 1955).
[88] *Supra* note 84, at 651.

it, since it gave added certainty that succession would be achieved.[89]

The Commission evidently does not wholly accept the implications of *Insurance Securities*. A former officer of the SEC argued:

> The view that what was involved in the *Insurance Securities* case was simply the "reinstatement" of service contracts with the approval of stockholders probably accounts for the court's refusal to accept the SEC position. The SEC view was that the transfer of control terminated the old contracts by virtue of Section 15(a)(4) and new contracts had to be negotiated between the investment company and the investment adviser. There was no such negotiation in the true sense. Obviously if fiduciaries acting solely in the interest of the security holders had negotiated a new contract on behalf of the investment company, rather than on behalf of the selling stockholders of the investment adviser, the excess of price over the book or asset value of the control stock would have inured to the benefit of the investors.[90]

Any notion that the SEC's apparent setback in *Insurance Securities* could serve to insulate the controversial relationship between investment companies and their investment advisers was soon dispelled by subsequent litigation, most of which centered around the fees paid by the funds for investment advice. While the fund and the adviser are separate entities, the adviser serves in a fiduciary capacity with respect to the fund; thus, it has been suggested that the customary identity between fund managements and their investment advisers inevitably involves conflicting loyalties. The fees paid by the fund to the investment adviser have usually been based on a percentage of net assets of the fund. Thus, if a mutual fund company with assets of $150 million or more (as some twenty-three companies had as early as 1958) paid advisory fees of 1 per cent of net assets, its annual disbursements for advisory services would exceed $1.5 million, plus expenses. The potential for unfairness seems apparent. In times of rising markets, the

[89] 72 HARV. L. REV. 1176, 1179 (1959).
[90] Greene, *Fiduciary Standards of Conduct Under the Investment Company Act of 1940*, 28 GEO. WASH. L. REV. 266, 277 (1959).

adviser can continue to benefit from increasing net assets while he sits back and does nothing. On the other hand, the further identity between investment advisers and the fund's principal broker in some cases results in "churning" or excessive portfolio turnover for the principal purpose of generating fees. It seems obvious that the costs of rendering advisory services do *not* increase proportionately with growth in net assets. In fact, as we have seen, as net assets rise, almost of necessity, the percentage of portfolio turnover decreases. Thus, relatively speaking, as the fund grows the adviser gets more for doing less. This factor—plus a number of law suits—has caused some funds to scale down the fees.

The service company fund problem arose, despite the statutory requirement that all service contracts be approved annually by a majority of fund directors who are not parties to the contract or by the fund shareholders at least every other year. The built-in check of independent directors has not been sufficient. In *Taussig v. Wellington Equity Fund, Inc.*[91] shareholders brought a derivative suit attacking the launching of a new company with the name "Wellington Equity Fund" as an act of unfair competition to Wellington Fund, one of the nation's four largest. Both funds were managed by the same investment adviser, the management of which had organized the new fund.

The court agreed. The property in the name "Wellington" belonged to the fund; the advisory service had already been well paid for any good will that may have been generated by its investment performance. Further, the adviser's breach of fiduciary responsibilities in organizing the second fund under the "Wellington" name gave rise to an *implied* private claim for relief, enforceable derivatively by a shareholder of Wellington Fund. It mattered not that the SEC under section 36 could have acted to enjoin the adviser for "misconduct" or "gross abuse of trust." Nor did it matter that the Investment Company Act does not specifically provide for a private right of action in such case. Rather, the court found an implied right to sue under the act, for the persons injured were of the very class the 1940 statute was designed to protect.

The application of this principle of the private right to sue for statutory wrong found expression again in *Brown v. Bullock*[92] in a

[91] 313 F.2d 472 (3d Cir. 1963), *cert. denied*, 374 U.S. 806 (1963).
[92] 194 F. Supp. 207 (S.D.N.Y. 1961); *aff'd*, 294 F.2d 415 (2d Cir. 1961).

charge of excessive advisory fees. Shareholders of Dividend Shares, Inc., an open-end fund, alleged that the investment fees paid by the fund management were excessive and constituted a gross abuse of trust (under section 36) and a conversion of the fund's assets (under section 37). Further, the complaint charged, the proxy statements for prior years were misleading, because they stated that the investment advisory arrangements with the fund were "similar to" those of five other funds managed by the same adviser, two of which, in fact, paid fees of one-fourth of 1 per cent of net assets, while the fund was charged one-half of 1 per cent of the first $100 million of net assets and one-fourth of 1 per cent of the excess.

The wrongs of excessive fees and misrepresentation, if true, voided the election of directors and their annual extension of the investment advisory contract, because the fund shareholders had been deprived of their right under the Investment Company Act to terminate the contract or seek its renegotiation. Without ruling on the truth of the allegations, the court of appeals for the Second Circuit held that the complaint stated a cause of action under the Investment Company Act.

With these rulings comes new hope that the most comprehensive of all the federal securities laws may yet form the base for effective enforcement of fiduciary standards of conduct in the investment company industry. If the requirement of "independent" directors turns out to involve a subjective realm in which judges cannot judge and lawmakers cannot legislate, if the Commission's powers of removal under section 36 are to be confined by the approach followed in *Insurance Securities*, there is still the vehicle of the private suit, which can be used to insure adherence to the fiduciary standards demanded by the act.

FOUNDATIONS

The accelerated growth, in size and numbers, of charitable foundations in recent years has been a subject of considerable controversy—even of congressional investigation. The reasons for this are many, but certainly the most important is the federal tax structure. Contributions to, and income received by, charitable foundations, even small "family foundations," are exempt from income taxation. In addition, contributions to a foundation, including the family foundation, can reduce the size of one's taxable estate, while control of the assets of the foundation may still remain with the donor.

Foundations are undoubtedly the *least* regulated of all institutional investors. Generally, there are no state laws that seriously impinge upon their freedom of action. Of course, in New York, for example, the Attorney General is empowered to bring an action to seize the assets of a foundation that is not administered in accordance with the purposes specified in its charter. But, as one might expect, this power is seldom exercised. For the most part only the broad provisions of the Revenue Code contain any real limitations. Briefly stated they are:

> (1) The foundation must be operated exclusively for "religious, charitable, scientific, testing for public safety, literary or educational purposes, or for the prevention of cruelty to children or animals. . . ."
>
> (2) No part of the net earnings may inure to the benefit of any private shareholder or individual.
>
> (3) No substantial part of the foundation's activities may be directed toward propaganda, legislative lobbying, or political contributions.[93]

The Revenue Code defines somewhat more precisely the limitations on private use of the assets of charitable foundations. Prohibitions are imposed on certain transactions involving the foundation, a substantial contributor of the entity's creator, his family, or any corporation controlled by him. Specifically, the foundation may not engage in any of the following arrangements without fear of losing its favored tax status: lending without adequate security and interest; paying excessively for personal services; making available foundation services on a preferential basis; paying more than adequate consideration for stock or property; selling its holdings for less than adequate consideration; engaging in any substantial diversion of the foundation's income or corpus.[94]

In addition, there are at least theoretical strictures on the amount of earnings and assets foundations may accumulate. Thus,

---

93 INT. REV. CODE OF 1954 § 501(c)(3).
94 INT. REV. CODE OF 1954 § 503(c)(1)-(6).

exemption can be denied if the amounts accumulated out of income (1) are unreasonable in amount or duration in order to carry out the charitable, educational, or other purpose or function constituting the basis for exemption, (2) are being used to a substantial degree for purposes or functions other than those constituting the basis for exemption, (3) are invested in such a manner as to jeopardize the carrying out of the charitable, educational, or other purpose or function constituting the basis for exemption.

The letter of the law, on its face, raises no barrier to either the individual or corporate transfer of stock to the foundation, which in turn may be staffed by self-perpetuating directors voting that stock as they see fit. Moreover, the income generated by the property held by the foundation may, within limits, be used to make additional stock purchases. Thus, foundations may and often do become instruments of corporate control.

What is more, as a practical matter foundations are but mildly inhibited by even the vague restraints of the tax law, for effective enforcement is generally lacking. From 1952 to 1962 the Internal Revenue Service failed to conduct a field audit of 433 foundations with combined assets of $8.6 billion. These included eleven Rockefeller-controlled foundations with a total value of $1,016,440,732 and eight Ford-dominated foundations with assets of $2.2 billion. Even where auditing took place, a congressional committee doubted its effectiveness.[95] It is in this context that foundation power and its exercise must be viewed. First, let us consider briefly the measure of economic concentration in foundations.

The recent exploratory studies of foundation impact on our economy was made by the House Small Business Committee in two reports during 1962/1963. Startling as some of the reports' findings may be, they but hint at the magnitude of foundation assets. The second study report states: "The Treasury Department has no more knowledge today, respecting the number of foundations in existence, than it had 15 years ago in 1948." What is more, declared the report, "Our findings of December 31, 1962 indicate that there may be countless foundations in operation without the knowledge of the Treasury."[96]

[95] CHAIRMAN'S REPORT TO THE HOUSE SMALL BUSINESS COMMITTEE, 88TH CONG., 1ST SESS., TAX-EXEMPT FOUNDATIONS AND CHARITABLE TRUSTS: THEIR IMPACT ON OUR ECONOMY x, 5-15 (Comm. Print 1963).
[96] *Id.* at 1.

Even without an accurate count, the increase in the sheer number of foundations was obvious. The year 1952 saw 12,295 tax-exempt organizations file the required revenue returns; this number grew to 45,124 by 1960. How much capital rests with these foundations perhaps is indicated by the aggregate size of a selected group of 534 studied by the committee:

> At the close of 1960, the 534 foundations under study held over $7 billion (at market value) in the stock of over 2,000 different corporations.
>
> One hundred eleven of those 534 foundations owned 10 per cent or more of at least one class of stock in one or more of 263 different corporations on December 31, 1960. The stock ownership of those 111 foundations ranged from 10 per cent to 100 per cent. . . .[97]

Illustrative of potential working control of corporations by foundations are the following: 15.4 per cent of the common nonvoting stock of Kaiser Industries Corporation is owned by Henry J. Kaiser Family Foundation, Oakland, California; 15.21 per cent of the common voting stock of Coca-Cola International is held by Emily & Ernest Woodruff Foundation, Atlanta, Georgia; 45.26 per cent of the common Class A voting stock of Eli Lilly & Co., by Lilly Endowment, Inc., Indianapolis, Indiana; 34 per cent of the capital voting stock of S. S. Kresge Co., by Kresge Foundation, Detroit, Michigan; 10 per cent of the preferred A voting stock of Pittsburgh Steel Co., by Donner Foundation, Inc., Philadelphia, Pennsylvania; 21.29 per cent of the common voting stock of the Sun Oil Co., by Pew Memorial Trust, Philadelphia, Pennsylvania; 11.69 per cent of the common voting stock of Hormel, Inc., by Hormel Foundation, Austin, Minnesota; and 23.4 per cent of the common stock of Ralston Purina Co., by Danforth Foundation, St. Louis, Missouri.[98]

Foundations can be more than passive instruments of corporate control. They can be used positively to further corporate ambitions. The foundation can provide a tax-shielded preferential source for new money far superior to other institutions. When Sears, Roebuck

[97] *Id.* at 1-2.
[98] *Id.* at 8-9.

& Co. needed a loan of $1.2 million, it went to the Sears, Roebuck Foundation and obtained the money at 3 per cent interest.

Still more significant is the use of a foundation to acquire control of other corporations. Examples are not lacking. On December 29, 1960, the J. M. Kaplan Fund, Inc., entered into the following stock exchange with the Albert A. List Foundation, Inc., Byram, Conn. The fund received 126,000 shares of Glen Alden for 54,000 shares of Endicott Johnson Corporation. Mr. Albert A. List found the Johnson stock important in his attempt to capture control of the corporation. It is interesting to note further that no capital gain or loss schedule appeared on the J. M. Kaplan 1960 tax return concerning the stock exchange.[99]

To take another example, consider the 1961 acquisition by the Ford Motor Company of the Philco Corporation. Under the terms of the merger, 1 million shares of Ford were to be exchanged for 4.1 million shares of Philco common stock. For the needed shares, the company went to the Ford Foundation, the holder of 89 per cent of the outstanding shares of the Ford Motor Company.

> The company paid the foundation $100,719,250 in cash for the stock, or $94.75 a share (Ford Motor Co. common stock closed at $98.875 on September 12, 1961, the day before the contract was executed), far above the $52 a share at which it was carried on the foundation's books. Nevertheless, this amounted to a retrieval, by the Ford family—through Ford Motor Co.—of a sizable portion of the contributions they had once made to the foundation. What is given, apparently, may sometimes be taken back. Of course, the foundation paid no capital gains tax on the double value of its Ford Motor Co. stock.[100]

SOME OBSERVATIONS ON THE NATURE OF PRESENT REGULATIONS

The web of state and federal regulation affecting the activities of institutional investors has been described, although in somewhat summary fashion. The power of the regulatory agencies is impressive. But we have also seen that this power is not always exercised.

---

[99] CHAIRMAN'S REPORT TO THE HOUSE SMALL BUSINESS COMMITTEE, 87TH CONG., 1ST SESS., TAX-EXEMPT FOUNDATIONS AND CHARITABLE TRUSTS: THEIR IMPACT ON OUR ECONOMY 81 (Comm. Print 1962).

[100] *Id.* at 82.

Our survey of insurance supervision and of the regulation (or lack of it) of foundations has illustrated this point.

Laws must be administered by men, who are capable of good as well as evil, of wisdom as well as vanity. It follows that the laws may be distorted, twisted to improper ends, or even ignored by those in authority, depending upon their character and ability. Thus, law becomes something more than what the courts—or the administrative agencies—will do in fact. The measure of a law depends in large part on the ability and integrity of the men who enforce it. Dean Padover wrote, "[G]overnment officers were not always eager to carry out the regulations. Often drawn from the business community, they carried that point of view with them into office."[101] To these men it was not unethical to read a regulatory law narrowly; government regulation, after all, was a violation of the private enterprise principle. The advice of Attorney General Richard Olney to his former employer, the president of the Chicago, Burlington and Quincy Railroad, is enlightening. (The letter was written by the Attorney General during the administration of President Cleveland concerning the railroads' fight to abolish the Interstate Commerce Commission.)

> My impression would be that looking at the matter from a railroad point of view exclusively, it [repeal] would not be a wise thing to undertake. . . . The attempt would not be likely to succeed; if it did not succeed . . . the result would very probably be giving it [the Interstate Commerce Commission] the power it now lacks. The Commission, as its functions have now been limited by the courts, is, or can be made, of great use to the railroads. It satisfies the popular clamor for government supervision of the railroads, at the same time that that supervision is almost entirely nominal. Further, the older such a commission gets to be, the more inclined it will be found to take the business and railroad point of view of things. It thus becomes a sort of barrier between the railroad corporations and the people and a sort of protection against hasty and crude legislation hostile to the railroad interests. . . . The part of wisdom is not to destroy the Commission, but to utilize it.[102]

[101] Padover, *Management and Government—The Balancing of Sovereignties*, 3 SOCIAL MEANING OF LEGAL CONCEPTS 262, 274 (1952).

[102] Quoted, *id.* at 274.

Some have argued that the prediction of the Attorney General has been fulfilled. In 1955 one scholar wrote: "The ICC has become an integral part of the railroad industry, and its record reflects its commitment to the welfare of that industry. Vitality and independence have petered out in the ICC."[103] The public no longer takes an interest in the work of the Commission. Apathy has set in; the fervor of the reform movement that gave birth to the ICC and permeated its activities has softened.

For the Securities and Exchange Commission, however, the momentum of the reform movement still carries forward. The days of the New Deal continue to be recalled. As an independent agency, the SEC is young and vigorous, while the ICC is old. Significant additions were made to the SEC's powers as late as 1940 with the passage of the Investment Company Act. New life has been breathed into the agency by the recent *Special Study of the Securities Markets* and the resulting adoption of the Securities Acts Amendments of 1964. Looking back, Mr. Justice Douglas, Chairman of the Commission during its early years, wrote of the SEC, "We had an able, earnest, and dedicated group of people administering these acts. We had youth and idealism on our side. . . . We were not concerned with ideas of personal gain or preferment."[104]

Though the work of the SEC has increased tremendously over the years, its staff of thirteen hundred employees is not very different in size from that maintained in its first year of operation. Only the appropriations to the Commission have increased from $1,545,337 in 1935 to $13,261,700 for fiscal 1963. In the latter year, the Commission collected over $2.5 million in fees; thus the net cost of operations was under $11 million.

> The SEC has attracted as members of the Commission and as members of its staff many outstanding personalities. A constantly rising market, an improvement in economic conditions, and the solution by the Commission of many of the numerous complex problems it has faced have required a high degree of ability and skill.[105]

[103] BERNSTEIN, REGULATING BUSINESS BY INDEPENDENT COMMISSION 90 (1955).

[104] Douglas, *Foreword to Securities and Exchange Commission Silver Anniversary Commemorative Symposium,* 28 GEO. WASH. L. REV. 5 (1959).

[105] Dean, *Twenty-Five Years of Federal Securities Regulation by the Securities and Exchange Commission,* 59 COLUM. L. REV. 697, 708 (1959).

Perhaps more than any other federal agency, the SEC's internal operations, and even the selection of Commission members, have been relatively free of political interference. Two of its five members, including the Chairman, are veterans of over twenty years' experience on the Commission's staff.

About three hundred attorneys and investigators are stationed in regional offices to check on the activity of registered security brokers and dealers and to investigate possible fraudulent acts in the securities markets.

> Inspections have been conducted on a test check basis following prescribed procedures. The regional office selects the firm to be inspected, although it is guided by inspection goals set forth by the Division of Trading and Exchanges [ed. now the Division of Trading and Markets] in the headquarters office. The staff appears to be alert to problems of investigation and has tried to improve investigatory techniques. The field inspectors have considerable knowledge of brokerage practices and seem to be highly regarded by the industry.[106]

Dedication alone is not the sole reason for the effectiveness of the SEC. Prodded by government, the industry has responded and voluntarily assumed a measure of responsibility. So it was that a former chairman of the SEC wrote:

> It is possible to argue that the disciplinary activities of the Commission, the "watchdog of Wall Street," have set the pace for the industry. The fact is, however, that the patterns of conduct and the standards of corporate morality, at one time so widely questioned and disputed but now followed uniformly, have more often than not become established by the voluntary action of responsible professional and business leaders. The pioneering work of industry and the bar in the framing of this new point of view has been followed by that of other thoughtful men who have evolved existing patterns of conduct based upon the principles of honesty, fair dealing, and full disclosure underlying the securities acts.
>
> Business and government have, in this field, arrived at a certain philosophical maturity. The responsibility of management to its stockholders and to the general public and the de-

---

[106] *Supra* note 103, at 238.

velopment of the concept that all business is to some degree
affected with a public interest may well be considered to represent the real contribution of the Securities and Exchange Commission to society during the quarter century just passed.[107]

For our purposes, therefore, the facts narrated in this chapter
culminate in a question. Are institutional investors ready to assume
responsibilities in their portfolio corporations commensurate with
their accumulated power? The governing agencies, either by law or
by choice, have not imposed such responsibilities. Rather, the regulators have been primarily concerned with the security of the institutions' beneficiaries: the insured, the depositor, and the shareholder.
Save for the SEC, none of the regulatory systems by which the institutions are governed is designed for the protection of even the institutions' shareholders, not to mention the interests of shareholders
of portfolio companies.

State insurance departments, by way of example, have demonstrated a singular disinclination to apply either antitrust or deceptive practice principles, although they have the statutory power to
do so. Their full efforts have been directed toward the maintenance
of solvency in the insurance industry, and thereby toward safe-
guarding the insured. Mergers and agreements in restraint of trade,
in the mind of the agencies, apparently are not relevant to meaningful industry regulation.

Yet, whether this attitude will remain fixed, whether institutional investors will themselves assume added responsibilities in the
absence of additional legislation, is another matter. To the extent
that institutions can no longer sell their holdings at will, to the extent that they realize the increasing unavailability of the Wall Street
Rule, the institutions will be forced to exert their influence upon
portfolio management. The signs of this recognition are already
present. Recall the statement of David Rockefeller, of the Chase
Manhattan Bank, that corporations will soon "find themselves dealing increasingly with these sophisticated investors," for institutional
investors "will become more demanding of management as time
moves on . . . especially if their holdings become so large that they
cannot readily or quickly liquidate their investments."[108]

[107] Gadsby, *Historical Development of the SEC—The Government View,* 28
GEO. WASH. L. REV. 6, 16 (1959).
[108] Address by David Rockefeller, "Business Enterprise and the Economy in

Yet, if the institutions do act, the consequences that may attach are as yet uncertain. Because of this, if nothing else, the institutions would probably prefer to have a course of accepted conduct delineated by the government. What they now can or should do is largely uncharted; danger looms large in the form of uncertain liabilities, but the price of continued inaction may prove too great. It may be this fear that caused some important representatives in the insurance industry to encourage the states to develop and exercise their expertise in the area of unfair competition.

the Next Ten Years," before the Special Conference for Financial Executives of the American Management Association at the Roosevelt Hotel, New York, October 14, 1958 (Mimeo) at pp. 4-5.

6

**SOME POSSIBLE
ANTITRUST ASPECTS:
THE STIGMA OF BIGNESS**

Institutional investors hold the power to check the managements of their portfolio corporations. Yet for the most part they have avoided using that power. "We are afraid to act," said an official of an institutional investor in an interview with one of the authors. "If the public became aware of the power we possess they might react against it." Bigness has long been tainted with distrust. The infamous comment of Cornelius Vanderbilt is recalled: "What do I care about law? Hain't I got the power?" Vast might held by a few men has always disturbed Americans. This was written of the year 1937:

> There are only ten sovereign states which have within their respective borders property valued at more than the assets of either the Metropolitan Life Insurance Co. or the American Telephone & Telegraph Company. Stated in another way, each of those two corporations is richer than any one of thirty-eight sovereign states.[1]

[1] Senator O'Mahoney, *The Preservation of Economic Freedom, Final Statement, Temporary National Economic Committee*, S. Doc. No. 39, 77th Cong., 1st Sess. at 677 (1941).

It matters not that the giant enterprise is efficient. The presumption is, where bigness approaches monopoly, that the enterprise, not the public, would enjoy the fruits of efficiency.

> [T]he efficiency of monopolies, even if established, would not justify their existence unless the community should reap benefit from the efficiency; experience teaches us that whenever trusts have developed efficiency, their fruits have been absorbed almost wholly by the trusts themselves. From such efficiency as they have developed the community has gained substantially nothing. . . . For instance: . . . *The Steel Trust,* a corporation of reputed efficiency. The high prices maintained by it in the industry are matters of common knowledge. In less than ten years it accumulated for its shareholders or paid out as dividends on stock representing merely water, over $650,000,000.[2]

In strong terms Mr. Justice Douglas, dissenting in *United States v. Columbia Steel,* argued against allowing the acquisition by United States Steel Corporation of Consolidated Steel Corporation. He grounded his argument on the potential of a few companies to determine steel prices, and the effect of their determination on the economy:

> Size in steel should therefore be jealously watched. In final analysis, size in steel is the measure of the power of a handful of men over our economy. That power can be utilized with lightning speed. It can be benign or it can be dangerous. The philosophy of the Sherman Act is that it should not exist. For all power tends to develop into a government in itself. Power that controls the economy should be in the hands of elected representatives of the people, not in the hands of an industrial oligarchy. Industrial power should be decentralized. It should be scattered into many hands so that the fortunes of the people will not be dependent on the whim or caprice, the political prejudices, the emotional stability of a few self-appointed men. The fact that they are not vicious men but respectable and social minded is irrelevant. That is the philosophy and command of the Sherman Act. It is founded on a theory of hostility

[2] BRANDEIS, THE CURSE OF BIGNESS, quoted by Mr. Justice Douglas, dissenting in United States v. Columbia Steel Co., 334 U.S. 495, 535, note 1 (1948),

to the concentration in private hands of power so great that only a government of the people should have it.[3]

The Law Applied to Bigness

It is more than the vague fear of possible restrictive legislation that restrains giant enterprises from openly using their power. There is the present danger that the antitrust laws, with their sweeping remedial provisions, will be used against them. The cases are replete with warnings against bigness; the dissent of Mr. Justice Douglas sometimes appeared to rise to the stature of the holding. In *United States v. Swift & Co.,* Mr. Justice Cardozo said:

> Mere size, according to the holding of this court, is not an offense against the Sherman Act unless magnified to the point at which it amounts to a monopoly . . . but size carries with it an opportunity for abuse that is not to be ignored when the opportunity is proved to have been utilized in the past.[4]

The Cardozo line of demarcation is near equivocal. As a rule of law it provides but an ethereal guide. In *United States v. United States Steel Corporation,* the Government directed its monopoly charge against the giant steel organization. The Court stated, "The Government, therefore, is reduced to the assertion that the size of the Corporation, the power it may have, not the exertion of the power, is an abhorrence to the law." Said the Court:

> The Corporation is undoubtedly of impressive size and it takes an effort of resolution not to be affected by it or to exaggerate its influence. But we must adhere to the law and the law does not make mere size an offense or the existence of unexerted power an offense.[5]

Exerted power is the needed element to condemn bigness. *United States v. Aluminum Company of America* provided an opportunity to define that element. A "natural monopoly" was the defense of the aluminum company to the Government's attack. The company pleaded that it was the passive beneficiary of its position. Judge Learned Hand replied:

[3] 334 U.S. 495, 536 (1948).
[4] 286 U.S. 106, 116 (1932).
[5] 251 U.S. 417, 450, 451 (1920).

It [the company] insists that it never excluded competitors; but we can think of no more effective exclusion than progressively to embrace each new opportunity as it opened, and to face every newcomer with new capacity already geared into a great organization, having the advantage of experience, trade connections and the elite of personnel. Only in case we interpret "exclusion" as limited to maneuvers not honestly industrial, but actuated solely by a desire to prevent competition, can such a course, indefatigably pursued, be deemed not "exclusionary." So to limit it would in our judgment emasculate the Act; would permit just such consolidations as as it was designed to prevent.[6]

Recently, however, the Court reviewed the *Aluminum* decision. Judge Hand, the Court held, did not mean to strike monopolies acquired by superior technical skill or effective competitive activities.[7] The Court refused to accept the Government's contention that only if monopoly power is thrust upon a defendant "by circumstances beyond his control" does it escape the antitrust laws. However, Justices Douglas and Black and the Chief Justice dissented.[8] The defendant, they urged, should have the burden of proving that it owes its monopoly *solely* to superior skill, an almost insurmountable burden. Further, the dissenting Justices pointed out, in the case at bar the defendant

sought and maintained dominance through illegal agreements dividing the world market, concealing and suppressing technological information, and restricting its licensee's production by prohibitive royalties, and through numerous maneuvers which might have been "honestly industrial" but whose necessary effect was nevertheless exclusionary.[9]

About all that can be learned from this brief statement of leading cases is that the ultimate meaning of bigness within the antitrust laws will depend to a large extent on the philosophical make-up of the judiciary. Some would, as a matter of law, consider

---

[6] 148 F.2d 416, 431 (2d Cir. 1945).
[7] U.S. v. E. I. duPont deNemours & Co., 351 U.S. 377 (1956).
[8] *Id.* at 414.
[9] *Id.* at 425.

bigness in itself a factor in an antitrust action. Others would look to bigness as an element which comes and sustains itself by any exertion of power. All would strike at bigness if coupled with acts of exertion which seek to restrain or lessen competition.

THE LAW OF BIGNESS APPLIED TO INSTITUTIONAL INVESTORS

Concentration characterizes the industry of the institutional investor. A relative few institutional investors possess much of the vast wealth held by all institutions. Moreover, these large enterprises frequently are encouraged not to compete unduly with each other. The result often is not mere neutrality but open cooperation between institutional investors to effect desired ends.

Section 10 of the New York Banking Law states:

> It is hereby declared to be the policy of the State of New York that the business of all banking organizations shall be supervised and regulated through the banking department in such manner as to . . . eliminate unsound and destructive competition among such banking organizations and thus to maintain public confidence in such business and protect the public interest and the interests of depositors, creditors, shareholders and stockholders.

Thus, unlimited competition is barred, as a matter of state policy, a policy which may be at variance with the federal government's view of the antitrust laws.

> For practical purposes, it seems necessary to assume as to all save the most local of banks, that their operations do or can fall within the area occupied by the Sherman Act—and to remember that the Department of Justice contends the Sherman Act is designed to apply to *all* interstate commerce capable of being dealt with under the Federal Constitution.
>
> What is the effect of state policy if it conflicts with the Sherman Act concept?
>
> Under settled antitrust law, state policy does have a field of application. Private parties making banking arrangements or agreements authorized and directed by state law, or giving effect to declared state policy, are protected, within limits, from antitrust prosecution. But the agreements must be in

fulfillment of a state-made policy—not merely a private policy which the state will accept.[10]

An analogous result was reached in the recent case of *Silver v. New York Stock Exchange*,[11] in which the Supreme Court faced the problem of accommodating the policies underlying both the Sherman act and the Securities Exchange Act of 1934. Under attack was an Exchange ruling that required member firms to discontinue private direct wire services previously extended to the plaintiffs, who were nonmember broker-dealers. The Exchange contended that the duties of self-regulation imposed by the Securities Exchange Act of 1934 necessarily exempted it from the antitrust laws, and refused to grant plaintiffs a hearing or even to state the reasons why it had ordered removal of private wire service to the plaintiffs. But the Court held that neither the duty of self-regulation nor the regulatory scheme empowering the SEC to review exchange action provided any blanket exemption from the application of antitrust principles. Removal of the private wire connections without sufficient justification derived from the Securities Exchange Act constituted a group boycott in violation of section 1 of the Sherman Act.

To resolve the question the Court imposed the requirement of notice and hearing upon the Exchange.

[I]t is clear that no justification can be offered for self-regulation conducted without provision for some method of telling a protesting nonmember why a rule is being invoked so as to harm him and allowing him to reply in explanation of his position. No policy reflected in the Securities Exchange Act is, to begin with, served by denial of notice and an opportunity for hearing. Indeed, the aims of the statutory scheme of self-policing—to protect investors and promote fair dealing—are defeated when an exchange exercises its tremendous economic power without explaining its basis for acting, for the absence of an obligation to give some form of notice and, if timely requested, a hearing creates a great danger of perpetration of injury that will damage public confidence in the exchanges.[12]

[10] Berle, *Banking Under the Antitrust Laws,* 49 COLUM. L. REV. 589, 596 (1949).
[11] 373 U.S. 341 (1963).
[12] *Id.* at 361. The implications of this case are great. In addition to the ex-

So it was that the Court reached an accommodation between a regulatory scheme embodied in the Securities Exchange Act of 1934 and the antitrust laws. This was not the first case in which attempts had been made to apply the antitrust laws to the securities industry. In *United States v. Morgan,* the government charged a few large investment banking houses with having a tacit understanding not to compete for the business of companies whose financing had traditionally been handled by one of their number. The result of such an understanding was to give the established house a monopoly in marketing the securities of the corporation with which it had previously done business. In sum, the government based its case on the theory that the defendants were dividing the market. The court held against the government. The practices of the industry were the result of a natural evolution to meet the needs of issuers. A "rule of reason" was applied to what was once thought of as a per se violation:

> [T]he history and development of the syndicate system as set forth in the preliminary portion of this opinion demonstrates that the modern syndicate system in general use today by the investment banking industry is nothing more nor less than a gradual, natural and normal growth or evolution by which an ancient form has been adapted to the needs of those engaged in raising capital. By no stretch of the imagination can it be considered a scheme or plan or device to which investment bankers have from time to time adhered.

>   *   *   *   *   *

> Despite all the general condemnation of price-fixing, I find nothing . . . which binds me to hold the clauses of these syndicate agreements now under attack to be illegal *per se* under the Sherman Act.[13]

The court in *Morgan* did not accept blanket assertions of "price-fixing" and "per se" violation. The nature of the price-fixing was inquired into. Did it stimulate rather than retard competition? This was the crucial question, which the court answered in the affirmative. This was the query that had to be posed if the court

changes the National Association of Securities Dealers may find itself subject to the holding.

[13] 118 F. Supp. 621, 686, 689 (S.D. N.Y. 1953).

was to follow *Board of Trade of the City of Chicago v. United States,* where Mr. Justice Brandeis declared:

> [T]he legality of an agreement or regulation cannot be determined by so simple a test, as whether it restrains competition. Every agreement concerning trade, every regulation of trade, restrains. . . . The true test of legality is whether the restraint imposed is such as merely regulates and perhaps thereby promotes competition or whether it is such as may suppress or even destroy competition. *To determine that question the court must ordinarily consider the facts peculiar to the business to which the restraint is applied; its condition before and after the restraint was imposed; the nature of the restraint and its effect, actual or probable.*[14] [Emphasis added.]

The rule of reason, an analysis of the facts, is the teaching of both the *Board of Trade* and *Morgan* decisions. Neither bigness itself nor the doing of an act in the abstract will constitute a violation of the antitrust laws. The importance of such a philosophy for the institutional investor is evident: Suppose a group of banks makes a loan to a corporation for the purpose of constructing a new plant. As a condition of the loan, the banks compel the corporation to have the plant constructed by Company A. This is done, not because the banks want to steer business to A, but because they want assurance that the work will be done well.

> Initially one would assume that a stipulation of this kind would not be an agreement in restraint of trade. Yet, were a practice adopted by banks requiring that all construction work done with money borrowed from them should be done by one of a small group of named engineers or contractors, thus giving this group a virtual monopoly on business so financed, such a practice might easily fall foul of the Sherman Act. *A bank undeniably has a clear right in respect of each individual transaction to make proper conditions looking toward the security and repayment: that is its business. Equally clearly it would seem that the bank must not use these provisions "unreasonably" to concentrate business in a few favored hands, and a*

[14] 246 U.S. 231, 238 (1918).

fortiori, *a number of banks would be forbidden to combine to produce this result.*[15] [Emphasis added.]

Thus, the use of massive power individually or collectively to control another business is suspect. Of this the Supreme Court has left no doubt. To the extent that the use of such power unduly restricts competition, it is more than suspect; it is clearly illegal. For institutional investors becoming increasingly entangled in portfolio corporations, there is a message and a warning in the Court's rulings.

Practically, financial institutions may be the object of a squeeze. They undoubtedly would prefer to purchase solely for "investment." By this they mean to buy and not vote corporate securities or to return their proxies to management. Yet this they may no longer be able to do so readily. As their holdings increase, it becomes difficult for them to follow the proposition, "If we don't like management, we'll sell." The market can absorb only a given amount of stock before prices slip downward. If a group of institutions have substantial holdings in the same company, the problem is further aggravated.

The alternative for the institutions is not comforting. It is a delicate, dangerous, and time-consuming task to attempt to influence the managements of portfolio corporations. At the very highest levels of business there are the links of friendship that could become strained. Similarly, the web of intercorporate relations exercises its own restraint. First, who the directors of the institution are may at the very least embarrass, if not stop, the institution from demanding corrective action by the portfolio corporation. Second, what is likely to be the attitude of a trust department that administers a pension fund for Corporation Y and annually purchases for that fund a given number of shares of that corporation? Will the trust department sell the stock if the investment seems in some danger? Will it dare to do anything that would depress the market for the shares of an important client, even though it may be in the interest of the fund?

Countervailing stresses may place the institutions in an ambivalent position. Even when it may be best for the institution to

---

[15] *Supra* note 10, at 603-04.

act, indecision springing from other loyalties may compel inaction. But this should not be tolerated as long as the stock held by the institution represents power. The automatic return of proxies to the management of a portfolio corporation is, in effect, a blank check. Endorsement is given for what has been and what will be. To this extent other shareholders are vitally affected by the institution that abdicates its role as shareholder.

A possible answer to the problem was suggested several years ago when some authorities urged that life insurance assets be freed for common stock purchases. Recognizing what might come from the entrance of such giants on the market, the same advocates suggested "sterilization," or the removal of voting rights, for stock held by life companies in portfolio corporations.

Sterilization as an alternative would at least serve the end of depriving management of supporting votes it might not deserve, while falling short, of course, of the more desirable goal of fiduciary standards of conduct for institutions *as shareholders*. There is, however, still another path, the broad contours of which have been shaped by the antitrust laws. As we have seen, standards of conduct are imposed either on individual or combined conduct which unreasonably restrains trade. As an example, view the purchase by E. I. du Pont de Nemours and Company of 23 per cent of the stock of General Motors during the years 1917 to 1919. From an investment standpoint, there seemed nothing improper in the purchase. The acquisition could be called neither a combination in restraint of trade, an attempt to monopolize, nor one that would tend to lessen competition.

What du Pont did with its holdings, however, presented another question. As early as 1917 the du Pont enterprise understood well the potential market in the auto industry for du Pont chemicals, paints, and varnishes. By 1921 Pierre S. du Pont was chairman of the board of both du Pont and General Motors. He, together with other du Pont officials, played a substantial role in insuring the sale to General Motors—up to the point of full production—of some of du Pont's products.

> Competitors did obtain higher percentages of the General Motors business in later years, although never high enough at any time substantially to affect the dollar amount of du

Pont's sales. Indeed, it appears likely that General Motors probably turned to outside sources of supply at least in part because its requirements outstripped du Pont's production. . . . For example, . . . General Motors took 93% of duPont's automobile Duco production in 1941 and 83% in 1946.

... [T]he bulk of duPont's production has always supplied the largest part of the requirements of the one customer in the automobile industry connected to duPont by a stock interest.[16]

For all of this, those who held high executive posts in du Pont and General Motors were honorable and fair men. Considerations of price, quality, and service were not overlooked by either corporation.

Pride in its products and its high financial stake in General Motors' success would naturally lead du Pont to supply the best. But the wisdom of this business judgment cannot obscure the fact . . . that du Pont purposely employed its stock to pry open the General Motors' market to entrench itself as the primary supplier of General Motors' requirements for automotive finishes and fabrics.[17]

The legal conclusion followed from the facts. Section 7 of the Clayton act condemns stock or asset acquisitions that are likely to lessen competition.

The statutory policy of fostering free competition is obviously furthered when no supplier has an advantage over his com-

[16] United States v. E. I. du Pont de Nemours & Co., 353 U.S. 586, 602, 604-07 (1957). The reluctance of Fisher Body to bow to duPont pressure should be noted. "Fisher Body was stubbornly resistant to duPont sales pressure. General Motors, in 1920, during Durant's time, acquired 60% stock control of Fisher Body Company. However, a voting trust was established giving the Fisher brothers broad powers of management. They insisted on running their own show and for years withstood efforts of high-ranking duPont and General Motors executives to get them to switch to duPont from their accustomed sources of supply. Even after General Motors obtained 100% stock control in 1926, the Fisher brothers retained sufficient power to hold out. By 1947 and 1948, however, Fisher resistance had collapsed, and the proportions of its requirements supplied by duPont compared favorably with the purchases by other General Motors Divisions."

[17] *Id.* at 606.

petitors from an acquisition of his customer's stock likely to have the effects condemned by the statute. . . . [T]he test of a violation of § 7 is whether, at the time of suit, there is a reasonable probability that the acquisition is likely to result in the condemned restraints. The conclusion upon this record is inescapable that such likelihood was proved as to this acquisition. The fire that was kindled in 1917 continues to smolder. It burned briskly to forge the ties that bind the General Motors market to du Pont, and if it has quieted down, it remains hot, and, from past performance, is likely at any time to blaze and make the fusion complete.[18]

The du Pont story does not end here. The Supreme Court found a violation, but the district court in Chicago was left with the task of fashioning a remedy. From the Government came a demand for total divestiture of du Pont's 23 per cent interest in General Motors. And from du Pont came a vehement response to this extreme remedy. To put such a quantity of stock on the market would seriously depress its price, thereby causing injury not only to du Pont and its shareholders but also to over 700,000 G.M. shareholders. On remand the district court, in a lengthy, careful opinion, issued an intricate injunction that would have sterilized voting power of du Pont's G.M. stock but would not have required divestiture.[19]

On a second trip to the Supreme Court, the district court was again reversed. Recognizing that even a court order can go only so far in controlling human conduct in the realm of continuing business relationships, the Court stated:

[A]n injunction can hardly be detailed enough to cover in advance all the many fashions in which improper influence might manifest itself. And the policing of an injunction would probably involve the courts and the Government in regulation of private affairs more deeply than the administration of a simple order of divestiture. We think the public is entitled to the surer, cleaner remedy of divestiture. The same result would follow even if we were in doubt. For it is well settled that once the Government has successfully borne the considerable burden

[18] *Id.* at 607.
[19] United States v. E. I. duPont deNemours & Co., 177 F. Supp. 1 (N.D. Ill. 1959).

of establishing a violation of law, all doubts as to the remedy are to be resolved in its favor.[20]

What the Supreme Court indicated in *du Pont* became clear in *United States v. First National Bank & Trust Company of Lexington*.[21] One enterprise, alone or in combination, may not acquire control over another if the effect may be substantially to lessen competition. It matters not that the acquiring corporation is engaged in a different line of business; the law is directed toward the effect on competition, not toward the nature of the parties. And, it must be emphasized, whether an acquisition has taken place is measured in terms of potential control, not legal abstractions. In the *du Pont* case, the acquisition of 23 per cent of General Motors' stock was clearly sufficient for this purpose.

For the institutional investors, the rule of the antitrust cases is this: The power they hold may be used to do what is reasonably necessary to protect and enhance their investments. This may even include, in extreme cases, agreeing among themselves to vote out an incompetent or dishonest management, or any lesser joint act that would serve to insure management fidelity to the portfolio corporation and all of its shareholders. But when institutional action operates to the detriment of all other shareholders of the portfolio concern, which may happen at times if the institution is a creditor as well as an equity holder, then questions of motivation properly become relevant.

Should one or more institutions attempt to influence the management of a portfolio corporation in a manner designed to lessen competition among institutions, the antitrust laws should immediately come into play. By the same token, if they use their power to restrain competition unduly among the portfolio concern and its competitors, the antitrust laws clearly should apply. In short, institutions should *use*, but not *abuse*, the power they hold.

Thus, a bank administering the du Pont pension fund may not purchase 23 per cent of General Motors' stock and then induce General Motors to buy paint from du Pont. And what the bank may not do for its beneficiary, it may not do for itself. The power of a trust department may not be invoked in such a manner to

[20] 366 U.S. 316, 334 (1961).
[21] 376 U.S. 665 (1964).

lessen competition between the institution's commercial division and other competing lenders. Management of a portfolio corporation should be free to seek money at the lowest possible price.

Beyond this, as shareholders, institutions should have an obligation to concern themselves with promoting a more profitable corporation. For example, it would seem altogether proper for an institution to encourage, and even insist, that a management continuity program be adopted by a portfolio concern. In such case the institution would be embarking on a course consistent with the preservation of its own interests as well as those of other shareholders in the portfolio corporation. There would be neither unreasonable restraint of trade nor any probable lessening of competition. Support for this proposition finds some analogy in other areas of antitrust law. In the area of tying agreements, recent court decisions have enunciated a doctrine that probably can best be described as the "business justification defense."

For example, tying agreements over the years have been frowned upon by the courts.[22] Under section 1 of the Sherman Act, it is an unreasonable restraint of trade to ask a man to buy a product he does not want in order to get one he does want. Indeed, the unfairness felt by the purchaser also is felt by those who would like to sell him a substitute for the tied product.

But despite the taint that attaches to tie-ins, there have been instances when the blemish was removed by business justification. Consider, by way of example, the case of Jerrold Electronics. It pioneered in the complex industry of community television antenna equipment. Purchasers of Jerrold equipment were required to take a Jerrold service contract. The exploring company could hardly do otherwise, for unfavorable consumer reaction due to improper maintenance might have destroyed the fledgling enterprise. Until the organization sank its roots and became established, the court allowed the tie-in.[23]

To an extent, business justification may be but another expression of a concept well known to the law, namely, the protec-

[22] United States v. Loew's, Inc., 371 U.S. 38 (1962); Brown Shoe Co. v. United States, 370 U.S. 294 (1962).

[23] United States v. Jerrold Electronics Corp., 187 F. Supp. 545 (E.D. Pa. 1960), aff'd mem., 365 U.S. 567 (1961). Yet after the business was entrenched the need for the tying agreement disappeared. Justification was lacking for any further insistence on the tie-in by Jerrold.

tion of good will. Long before statute, good will represented a right protected by the courts. Within bounds, the businessman could reasonably expect the judiciary to protect the fruits of his labors. If, for example, he installs a gasoline pump bearing his mark at a service station, he may demand that the station operator use only his gasoline—for the public believe that they are buying the markholder's gasoline, not that of someone else.[24]

Like the businessman concerned with preserving the good will of his enterprise, the institutional investor must safeguard its investment. Toward this end the antitrust laws should present no barrier, so long as the institution acts within the bounds of reason and the doctrine of business justification.

Immediately the question arises: What can the financial institution do to promote its interests that will not, at the same time, unjustifiably damage those of other shareholders in the portfolio company, or unduly lessen competition? While we do not attempt to delineate all areas of potential action, one such course has already been suggested: insistence upon adequate programs to insure continuity of qualified management. For several reasons this is selected: (1) It is vital to the long-term well-being of a corporation. (2) At least some of the regulatory agencies have had experience in ascertaining the effectiveness of management succession programs. (3) It in effect represents no more than the responsible exercise of the corporate franchise that is the privilege—nay, the obligation—that attends significant stock ownership by institutions.

Specifically, the 1960 Bank Merger Act requires the Comptroller of the Currency, the Federal Reserve Board, or the Federal Deposit Insurance Corporation, in weighing approval of any bank merger, to pass upon the general character of management of both the acquired and the acquiring banks.[25] In the abstract one commentator found great difficulty with the management factor. To him it was vague, incapable of being objectively examined.

> How, for example, is the adequacy of management to be measured? By past performance? Reputation? The assertions of proponents of a merger? Assuming that a bank management is weak, how are the supervisory authorities to appraise the

[24] Federal Trade Commission v. Sinclair Refining Co., 261 U.S. 463 (1921).
[25] 12 U.S.C. § 1828(c) (1963 ed., Supp. IV).

efforts of existing management to improve management quality, especially when the merger route is justifiable assuming the continued existence of inadequate management? And how is a presently weak management to be weighed against a permanent structural change brought about by a merger? This will all be a matter of arbitrary judgment on the part of the bank supervisory agencies. . . . Inclusion of the "banking factors" assures that a supervisory authority looking for a reason to approve a merger will find one.[26]

Adequacy of provisions for management continuity, however, can be assessed. It is, after all, a matter of business judgment with which businessmen deal every day. Every merger, acquisition, or disposition of a business as a going concern involves the exercise of this judgment. The institutions themselves are not unfamiliar with the concept. The controls typically obtained by lenders in private placements are frequently designed for just this purpose. As a recent example, a few years ago Trans World Airlines was in need of cash to finance its program of conversion to jet aircraft. The situation was desperate because TWA was already behind other major airlines in obtaining jet planes. A group of institutions provided the needed funds, over $300 million, but they demanded a heavy price. They insisted on voting control of the corporation, over 70 per cent of the stock of which was owned by Howard Hughes. The institutions thereupon installed their own management, and the company is now back in the black. From all indications, the way is not yet wholly clear for Mr. Hughes to oust the institutions' appointed management and regain voting control of the company. While the Civil Aeronautics Board ruled that Hughes's stock could be returned to him if he first divested himself of control of another airline, Hughes's right to regain control of TWA is still being disputed in the federal courts.

Under the Bank Merger Act, the regulatory agencies are obligated to take steps to insure sustained quality bank management, for without this the solvency of banks would be jeopardized. In a substantial number of mergers approved by the Federal Re-

[26] Herman, *The Philadelphia Bank Merger Decision and its Critics*, 1 THE NATIONAL BANKING REVIEW 391, 402-03 (1964).

serve Board the reason given was the failure of the acquired bank to provide for management continuity.

The recent take-over of two banks on the same day by the Chemical Bank New York Trust Company provides an indication of the problem and the capacity of "giant" banks. Chemical on December 20, 1963, had deposits of $4.558 billion. It sought prior approval of the asset acquisition and assumption of deposit liabilities of The Bensonhurst National Bank, which had deposits of $35 million.

Favoring the merger, the Federal Reserve Board stated:

Bensonhurst Bank is next to the smallest of the four commercial banks operating entirely in Brooklyn, which range in deposit size from $22.6 million to $113 million.

The financial condition of Bensonhurst Bank is sound, it has a strong capital structure, and its earnings have been consistently above average for banks of comparable size in the Second Federal Reserve District. However, the bank has been operated virtually as a "one-man-bank" under the dominance of its president, who is past normal retirement age, and problems inherent in this type of management have emerged. . . .

The prospects of developing from the bank's present staff successor management of comparable ability are not favorable, and efforts to recruit and retain successor executive personnel have been unsatisfactory. Thus, upon the president's withdrawal from active participation in the bank's affairs, certain problems of supervision can be anticipated, and it appears probable that the bank would lose at least part of the deposits he has attracted to it, particularly those of customers who no longer reside or conduct their business in the Bensonhurst and Flatbush areas served by the bank's two offices. In the circumstances, it seems probable that a smoother transition can be effected through the presence of competent successor management supplied by Chemical.[27]

Governor Robertson dissented from this view, however. It may be, he argued, that Bensonhurst had weak management. But,

[27] *In the Matter of Chemical Bank New York Trust Company, New York, New York,* 50 FED. RESERVE BULL. 321, 322 (Feb. 17, 1964).

with effort and with encouragement, perhaps from the board, new and competent young managers could be found. After all, Bensonhurst was an "A-1 institution with deposits of $35 million."[28]

The second bank taken over by Chemical was The First National Bank of Mount Vernon, New York, with deposits of $48.8 million. Giving its approval, the board stated:

> First National, chartered in 1889, has been operated since the turn of the century by the family which still holds a stock interest representing effective control of the bank. Its financial condition is sound and its capital structure adequate. However, while management is competent, and earnings prospects generally favorable, certain aspects of the bank's present posture led to the present proposal. With a concept of banking formed in a more spacious era, content to follow practices which were appropriate then, but are less than adequate now, executive management of the bank has aged without adapting to a changing community environment. Each of the two principal figures in management is now over seventy years of age. No preparation has been made for management succession, and there are no probable replacements in the present organization. With the controlling stock interest involved in the administration of an estate since the death within the past year of the former president, it is unlikely that efforts to recruit successor management would be successful. Accordingly, the management succession problem, while not acute at present, could become so at any time. In the context of the failure of present management to compete aggressively with The County Trust Company ("County Trust"), the largest Westchester County bank, and despite the protection enjoyed because of the "home office" feature of New York State law (which prevents establishment of de novo branches in Mount Vernon of banks headquartered elsewhere), unresolved management succession might well lead to declining profitability of the bank.[29]

A management continuity program might well have saved these banks from extinction through merger. The means could have been available to provide sustained quality management. Survival

[28] *Id.* at 324.
[29] *Id.* at 326.

of the corporate entity need not have rested on the fragile life of a single human being.

For financial institutions the analogy to be drawn from the Bank Merger Act is not obscure. To urge portfolio corporations to establish management continuity programs is both legally safe and practically feasible. It is the program, not the particular individual, with which the institutions would be concerned. While the antitrust laws clearly should limit institutional action with respect to portfolio corporations, the realm of permissible exercise of admitted economic power is still very broad. Standards of fair play may be vague, but they have, after all, been employed to govern human conduct for a good many centuries. The antitrust ethic attacks only the *unreasonable* restraint of trade. Thus, the basis for institutional inactivity cannot rest solely on restraints imposed by the antitrust laws. The prohibitions of the antitrust laws are not so broad or so vague as truly to inhibit institutions from developing appropriate standards of conduct for using the powers they hold, instead of abandoning them.

The crucial question, of course, is: What are appropriate standards of conduct and how are they to be developed? To the extent that institutions, as dominant shareholders, are deemed fiduciaries with respect to their portfolio companies and the other shareholders in such companies, we are not entirely lacking in precedents. It seems perfectly clear that a director of an institution who is, let us say, a building contractor, should not use his position to cause the institution to withhold financing for a competing contractor.

On the other hand the establishment of a management continuity program, at the insistence of powerful institutional shareholders, would represent the exact antithesis of the prevailing institutional practice of slavishly returning proxies to incumbent managements. The founding of such a program might be but one form of institutional action that could produce management leaders of proven merit without involving financial institutions in the daily operations of their portfolio corporations. Following this course, institutions could fulfill at least a portion of their obligations to shareholders of portfolio corporations while, at the same time, keeping well within the limits of the antitrust laws.

7

꧶꧶꧶꧶꧶꧶꧶

POWER AND
RESPONSIBILITY

In the preceding chapters we have delineated the emerging position of institutional investors as the dominant shareholders of American businesses. Their standing today as our largest shareholders is but an indication of what tomorrow may bring, for the power of institutions relative to that of individual shareholders is increasing at a remarkable pace. Institutions will hold nearly one-third of all New York Stock Exchange listed securities by 1970, and beyond that there is no reason to assume that the accumulation will stop at 40, 50, or even 60 per cent. The Exchange itself, perhaps in an effort to ignore a problem destined to draw increasing attention from lawyers, economists, businessmen, and perhaps ultimately the courts, has suggested that the trend toward institutional accumulation will soon level off, while admitting that the market by 1970 will be "vastly different" from what it is today.

That difference in part will be but a reflection of the state of our "affluent society." As the nation's per capita productivity increases, a greater portion of earned wealth will continue to be translated into savings that, in turn, are invested in the nation's business. While individual savings continue to seek new channels and assume an increasing variety of forms, they are all, by and large, in the hands of the institutions. The statistics already summarized bear this out. The magnitude of the country's accumulated savings is impressive. Holdings of the pension trust for New York City employees alone, for example, are nearly $4 billion.

We have also observed the power, influence, and expertise that accompany the mounting shareownership by institutions. At the same time, we have examined the extent and nature of existing legal controls on institutions. They are intricate but for the most part conceived in another era, when institutional controls were rightly concentrated on the objectives of insured solvency and the protection of individuals' savings from the catastrophic results of fraud and complete business failure in time of cyclical depression. The felt necessities of a more affluent society may justify other legitimate objectives for the developing ethics of institutional controls. In business we have long recognized that economic power carries with it responsibilities with respect to the use of that power. So, too, dominant economic power may rightly entail increased responsibilities. Our purpose now is to examine the theoretical basis for increasing responsibilities of institutions *as shareholders*.

At one time it was said that corporations could contribute funds to charities only if a present business purpose were served. Charity for the benefit of the general welfare was ruled ultra vires; profits were for corporations, viz., the shareholders. This doctrine was promulgated when public corporations were relatively small and controlled but a fraction of the nation's wealth. The doctrine was also enunciated at a time when support for charitable institutions could more properly be considered a matter of private philanthropy, rather than public necessity. With the passing of years a new set of conditions arose. The court in *A. P. Smith Mfg. Co. v. Barlow* had to reexamine the theory of ultra vires and charitable contributions. It stated:

> When the wealth of the nation was primarily in the hands of individuals they discharged their responsibilities as citizens by donating freely for charitable purposes. With the transfer of most of the wealth to corporate hands and the imposition of heavy burdens of individual taxation, they have been unable to keep pace with increased philanthropic needs. They have therefore, with justification, turned to corporations to assume the

modern obligations of good citizenship in the same manner as humans do.[1]

To support its result the court held that a charitable grant for the maintenance of a university *did* serve a corporate purpose. "[I]ndeed, if need be the matter may be viewed strictly in terms of actual survival of the corporation in a free enterprise system."[2] The court accepted what scholars had reasoned earlier:

> Seventy years ago virtually every aspect of our society was favorable to private enterprise, business profits and political and economic freedom. For a board of directors at that time to have spent money for the avowed purpose of preserving the free enterprise system must have seemed an act of arrant folly. . . . Today, . . . economic as well as political freedom is in jeopardy.[3]

The law would not long arrest the development of corporate giving:

> The genius of our common law has been its capacity for growth and its adaptability to the needs of the times. Generally courts have accomplished the desired result indirectly through the molding of old forms. Occasionally they have done it directly through frank rejection of the old and recognition of the new. But whichever path the common law has taken it has not been found wanting as the proper tool for the advancement of the general good.[4]

As individuals in the past could support the felt needs of private charitable causes, shareholders could better protect themselves in the small corporation. They had both the capability and the desire to understand the affairs of the company. There was no necessity for one shareholder to safeguard another's interest; each looked after his own property. However, with the growth of the corporation in size and complexity and the wide distribution of shareownership, the reality of self-protection became a fiction. Only the informed,

---

[1] 98 A.2d 581, 585-86 (N.J.), *cert. denied*, 346 U.S. 861 (1953).

[2] *Id.* at 586.

[3] deCapriles and Garrett, *Legality of Corporate Support to Education: A Survey of Current Developments,* 38 A.B.A.J. 209, 210 (1952).

[4] *Supra* note 1, at 586.

powerful shareholders could fend for themselves. As an influence in the corporation, the large shareowners have been better able to obtain, analyze, and act on information to protect their economic interests. At times they have enhanced their own position at the expense of the uninformed, smaller shareholders. The courts were then faced with the question of whether the law could countenance the exploitation of the smaller owners by the larger, dominant shareholders.

The classic case of *Insuranshares Corp. v. Northern Fiscal Corp.* made a preliminary inquiry into the problem. A group of banks holding a minority but controlling interest in a corporation sold their stock to a group bent on looting the company. In determining the liability of the banks to the corporation, the court stated that those who control a corporation owe some duty to it when they transfer control to outsiders.

> The law has long reached the point where it is recognized that such persons may not be wholly oblivious of the interests of everyone but themselves, even in the act of parting with control, and that, under certain circumstances, they may be held liable for whatever injury to the corporation [is] made possible by the transfer.[5]

Defining the duty of the banks in "minimum terms," the court held those who sold control liable. As prudent men they were aware of the surrounding circumstances, of the possibility that the corporation would be robbed by the purchasers: "Specifically, the banks, with all their credit facilities made absolutely no investigation of the financial standing and resources of the purchasers and at no time received any information to indicate to them that the purchasers had any money whatever."[6]

The liability imposed by the court was not the amount of the premium paid for the defendants' stock. The damages were measured "by the difference in dollars between the assets of the plaintiff before the acts complained of and those found remaining at the time of the suit."[7] The court rejected the plea that the individual share-

[5] 35 F. Supp. 22, 25 (E.D. Pa. 1940).
[6] *Id.* at 27.
[7] 42 F. Supp. 126, 128 (E.D. Pa. 1941).

holders might be placed in a better position financially than they were prior to the diversion of the company's assets.

The theory upon which the defendants were brought to account was grounded in principles of tort: "If the facts indicate, or should put the seller on notice, that the transfer of control will injure the minority shareholders, there is liability for the harm thus caused."[8] The stronger shareholders may not exploit the weaker. The cases and the commentators are in agreement on this.

The *Insuranshares* decision provided the foundation for the development of the Doctrine of the Dominant Shareholder. It was relatively easy for the courts to stop one shareholder from harming another. But what could be done when the stronger shareholder profited solely because of his strength without any direct injury to the weaker? Could the courts entirely throw off the rule that one shareholder owes no fiduciary duty to another?

> The conventional approach is predicated upon the notion that the corporation—the collective body of shareholders—is a separate and distinct legal entity, an artificial personality, to whom an officer, a director or a controlling shareholder owes his sole duty. It follows as a corollary that the controlling shareholder is not a fiduciary of and owes no duty to the outside shareholders as individuals when he sells his stock to strangers.[9]

In *Levy v. Feinberg* the court spelled out what seemed to be the extent of the *Insuranshares* rule:

> [I]t is well settled that a director-majority stockholder can be compelled to account to the corporation for an improper sale of his stock; (1) Where in addition to the purchase price, he receives a bonus for relinquishing either his control or his office; (2) Where by a sale of his stock at a premium, he conspires fraudulently to turn over control to purchasers who mismanage the corporation; and (3) Where, without adequate investigation, he negligently turns over control to purchasers who pay him a bonus for the sale of his stock, and the purchasers then proceed to loot the corporate assets. In short, he can be com-

---

[8] deCapriles and Prunty, *Corporations*, 31 N.Y.U. L. REV. 490, 499 (1956).
[9] Jennings, *Trading in Corporate Control*, 44 CALIF. L. REV. 1, 6 (1956).

pelled to account where he receives a gain which can reasonably be traced to an abuse of his controlling position.[10]

The lines drawn in *Insuranshares* and *Feinberg*, however, were enlarged in *Perlman v. Feldmann* to establish a new proposition: Controlling shareholders *do* owe a fiduciary duty to their fellow shareholders. They must account for profits received in selling their "control" even though no injury is directly traceable to the corporation. Specifically, the *Perlman* case involved the following facts. The corporation, a marginal producer of steel, financed capital improvements through interest-free advances from end-users of steel in exchange for firm commitments for steel deliveries in a tight market. During the Korean War, a tight market period, the controllers, holding approximately one-third of the corporation's stock, sold out to a group of end-users who wanted to insure their source of steel supply. Actual control was transferred by the successive resignations of the incumbent directors and the replacing of them by the buyers' nominees. The price paid to the controllers nearly doubled the over-the-counter value of the shares. Though framed derivatively, minority shareholders sought individual relief for the sale of a corporate asset. The asset was the power to allocate steel; the premium paid for the defendants' stock over the market value, they claimed, represented the value of the asset. The "corporate asset" theory had been propounded in 1932 by Berle and Means in *The Modern Corporation and Private Property:* "[T]he power going with 'control' is an asset which belongs only to the corporation; and . . . payment for that power if it goes anywhere, must go into the corporate treasury." Nevertheless, the trial court denied recovery.[11]

The appellate court reversed; both as a director and dominant shareholder, Feldmann was held to stand in a fiduciary relationship to the corporation and to the minority shareholders.[12] The sale was termed a sacrifice of an element of the corporation's good will with unusual profit to the fiduciary who caused the sale. Further, the court stated, "The corporate opportunities of whose misappropriation the minority shareholders complain need not have been an ab-

[10] 29 N.Y.S.2d 550, 556 (1941).
[11] BERLE AND MEANS, THE MODERN CORPORATION AND PRIVATE PROPERTY at 243 (1932). 129 F. Supp. 162 (D. Conn. 1952).
[12] 219 F.2d 173 (2d Cir. 1955), *cert. denied,* 349 U.S. 952 (1955).

solute certainty in order to support this action against Feldmann. If there was a possibility of corporate gain, they are entitled to recover."[13] The court seemed to adopt the thesis of Berle and Means: The power attached to control is an asset belonging only to the corporation. Yet the court cautioned: "We do not mean to suggest that a majority stockholder cannot dispose of his controlling block of stock to outsiders without having to account to his corporation for profits or even never do this with impunity when the buyer is an interested customer, actual or potential, for the corporation's product."[14] While the "corporate asset" theory has elicited strong opposition, there is little question today that the law has evolved from the principles of tort to the fiduciary concepts of equity. The old rule of absolute freedom of action among shareholders has been discarded.

The analogy of the dominant shareholder to the institutional investor is this: The institutional investors have not yet acquired all the characteristics of the controllers, but they do have some. They possess large blocks of stock, which can strongly influence, if not ultimately determine, management action. They have the ability, the expertise, to evaluate management intelligently. They have the financial resources which management seeks for its capital needs and which can be brought to bear, if necessary, against management. In sum, the institutional investors are in a position to check corporate management. To that extent they are in the position of the controllers. The Doctrine of the Dominant Shareholder places the controller in a fiduciary relationship to minority shareholders; it also provides the theory for suggesting that the institutional investors should act to check corporate management for the benefit of themselves, their own shareholders, and other shareholders in the portfolio concern.

The Doctrine of the Dominant Shareholder has advanced the law a step toward the legal recognition of the realities of corporate democracy. Most shareholders are not in a position to fend for themselves; they cannot protect their property. Those who can protect themselves may undertake, either actively or passively, the role of *commissaires de surveillance* of management. But, for the most part, only the institutions are in a position to exert effective power in the

[13] *Id.* at 176-77.
[14] *Id.* at 178.

interest of preserving their investment. They hold indirectly through their financial resources, and directly through the vote, the power to influence management, although in most cases we have seen that that power is not affirmatively exercised. Of course, nonexercise does not abrogate the power; it simply goes by default to entrench incumbent management. Those who hold power must account for the results, whether they employ it affirmatively or, through nonaction, allow it to be used by others. Thus, the dominant shareholder theory recognized that "the function of control is to choose a management. This choice must be responsibly exercised. Though the courts are just beginning to enunciate this rule, businessmen of course understand it quite well, though they would probably deny that breach of the standard entails liability."[15]

By another analogy, the institutional investors are much like voting trustees in any of their portfolio corporations. They have the sole power to vote the shares they hold; the equitable owners of those shares, however, are the shareholders or beneficiaries of the institutional investors who, in turn, may number in the millions. By definition, a voting trust is simply a device whereby persons who own stock with voting powers divorce the voting rights from the ownership but retain the other economic benefits of ownership, including in most cases the power to dispose of the stock at will. The power to vote, however, is transferred to trustees in whom the voting rights of all depositors in the trust are pooled.

Voting trusts are almost universally permitted now by statute with the sole limitation usually being the duration of the trust. In New York, for example, a voting trust cannot last longer than ten years, subject to renewal, and all shareholders must be permitted to join the trust and deposit their shares. However, even in the absence of statute this device was permitted in many jurisdictions. The only condition imposed prior to statutory legitimation was that the trust must not seek to achieve an improper goal. This, of course, left a great deal to be defined which, by legislative edict, today no longer concerns the courts. Yet it is worth noting that one illustration of an improper goal was a voting trust created to guarantee management continuity without being connected to a special business purpose.

Before the legislature preempted the field, some courts held a voting trust to be illegal per se; its goal was not material. In *Warren*

---

[15] Berle, *"Control" in Corporate Law*, 58 COLUM. L. REV. 1212, 1220 (1958).

v. Pim[16] the court considered a voting trust designed "to insure a consistent and conservative management of the Fisheries Company in accordance with the views primarily of the British Stockholders, but for the general benefit of all other stockholders as well." With powerful language, Mr. Justice Pitney lashed out at the trust device:

> How such a purpose and effect can be seriously attributed to this masterpiece of professional ingenuity, which confides absolute and uncontrolled discretion to a group of inexperienced individuals who live remote from the scene of the company's activities, and whose personal stake in the success of the company is so insignificant that it may be disregarded entirely for practical purposes . . . I confess I am at a loss to imagine.[17]

The spark that consumed the voting trust in *Warren v. Pim* was ignited, in part, by nontrust members, other shareholders, who had elected not to become part of the pooled body. The court permitted them both to challenge the trust and to obtain relief from it. It stated: "Non-assenting parties are manifestly entitled to relief against it [a voting trust adjudged void]. And assenting parties, or those claiming under them, are clearly under a duty to withdraw at the first opportunity from any agreement that violates the letter or policy of the law."[18] The reasoning underlying the conclusion is clear. Shareholders live in the same corporate community. One cannot conspire to benefit at the expense of others. When a shareholder's interests are affected by the combined action of other shareholders, he may move against the combine.

While pressures of various kinds may have joined to convince the legislatures that voting trusts are not the evil monsters they were once made out to be, the principles by which the device was struck down were not entirely lost. Indeed, voting trusts are still prohibited by the rules of the New York Stock Exchange. However appropriate the voting trust may be in the small or family-held company, the Exchange's firm position is based on the idea that such devices have no place in a publicly held corporation. Whatever view one may take of shareholder democracy, such a bald isolation of ownership from control will not be tolerated.

[16] 59 ATL. 773 (N.J. 1904).
[17] *Id.* at 781-82.
[18] *Id.* at 779.

The analogy, then, becomes obvious. Institutional investors in fact are much like voting trustees of the stock of their portfolio corporations. The law, through decisions antedating the Doctrine of the Dominant Shareholder, once imposed real duties on the trustees as an essential condition for the continued existence of the trust. In addition, it allowed nonassenting shareholders to move against the trust when they were wrongfully affected by actions of the trustees. In legal contemplation, the theory again suggests that the institutional investor should act to aid in creating and maintaining responsible management in their portfolio corporations. For the institutional investor to say that it does not act and, therefore, does not hurt, misses the point. Nonaction to the institutional investor is a positive kind of action, where it means automatic support of management so long as it is an investor. To a significant extent, institutional investors can and do provide the means for the solid entrenchment of corporate management. By so doing, they profoundly affect the rights of other shareholders. They should, accordingly, be responsible for their actions.

The doctrines of the dominant shareholder and the voting trust are legal recognition of the principle that the privilege of power carries with it the duty of responsibility. This principle, it seems, is applicable to institutional investors today, and may well provide the theoretical roots for the imposition of future specific duties. The measure of those duties will be in relation to the power position of any one institution in any one corporation. The law will develop only in the light of the facts on a case-by-case basis. It is not possible, nor is it desirable, to delineate the future course of the law affecting relations among institutional investors, their portfolio companies, and other shareholders in such companies. Yet the following possibilities may be mentioned.

The facts will show that institutional investors are in a position to obtain and trade upon private information given them by the managements of their portfolio corporations. Seeking whatever news management may dispense often is the sole task of certain institutional employees. Obtaining the news adds to the institution's supposed expertise, its ability to make prudent investments. The extent to which managements will discuss corporate plans or reveal corporate projects undoubtedly depends in large part on the power and prestige of the institution. On the other hand, most shareholders would have neither the desire nor the time to make effective use of the same data given the institutions. Yet the point still holds that the institutions can and probably do profit from this data to the exclusion of other shareholders—and sometimes to the detriment of other investors. The future probably will find this institutional pattern of maintaining direct contacts with management emphasized as institutional holdings mount.

If the past is a guide to the future, one may expect certain restraints to be placed on the use by institutions of inside information. In *Oliver v. Oliver* the defendant, the president and director of an oil company, purchased the stock of the plaintiff without disclosing that the company's plant was to be sold at a price that would have substantially increased the value of the stock. The president-director argued that while he might have been a trustee for the corporation, he did not occupy the same status in relation to individual shareholders and therefore could trade as he liked with the plaintiff. The court answered:

> It is a matter of common knowledge that the market value of shares rises and falls, not only because of an increase or decrease in tangible property, but by reason of real or contemplated action on the part of managing officers; upon declaring or passing dividends; upon the making of fortunate or unfortunate contracts; the loss or gain of property in dispute; on profitable or disadvantageous sales or leases. And to say that a director who has been placed where he himself may raise or depress the value of the stock, or in a position where he first knows of facts which may produce that result, may take advantage thereof, and buy from or sell to one whom he is directly representing without making a full disclosure, and putting the stockholder on an equality of knowledge as to these facts, would offer a premium for faithless silence, and give a reward for the suppression of truth.[19]

So, too, the court in *Stewart v. Harris* stated: "The managing officers of a corporation are not only trustees in relation to the corporate entity and the corporate property, but they are also to some extent and in many respects trustees of the corporate shareholders."[20] Applying the rule, the court would not permit a president-director

---

[19] 45 S.E. 232, 234-35 (Ga. 1903); see also LOSS, SECURITIES REGULATION 1447 (2d ed. 1961).

[20] 77 Pac. 277, 279 (Kan. 1904).

of a bank to keep the bargain in a stock purchase. The president told the seller that the bank was in good condition, but he did not tell the seller just how good. And promptly after the sale the president had a 120 per cent dividend declared, the first in two years.

Other courts reached the same result as the *Oliver* and *Stewart* decisions through the evolution of the dialectic "Special Facts Doctrine." First verbalized by the Supreme Court in *Strong v. Repide,* the facts concerned nondisclosure of vital information in purchasing shares from the plaintiff. Again the defendant was an officer and director of the company as well as its major shareholder. The Court recognized the defendant's legal obligation to disclose those facts which would have altered materially the sale of stock. The reasoning of the Court did not lie in the abstract realm of director's liability. Rather, it was grounded in the power the defendant possessed:

> That the defendant was a director of the corporation is but one of the facts upon which the liability is asserted, the existence of all the others in addition making such a combination as rendered it the plain duty of the defendant to speak. He was not only a director, but he owned three-fourths of the shares of its stock, and was at the time of the purchase of the stock, administrator general of the company, with large powers.[21]

The ground has been substantially cut from under those precedents, once recognized as the majority view, which held that a director was not a trustee with respect to the corporation's shareholders. Professor Loss commented: "It seems fair to conclude from all this that the so-called 'majority' view is gradually giving way to the generally growing feeling of responsibility of corporate insiders—the development of a status of 'trusteeship' in a nontechnical sense."[22]

Yet the common law moves slowly. While the ethics of conduct may be verbalized, the specific duties that arise from them may only become apparent from the peculiar facts of litigated cases. Though the law plods an interstitial course, one would expect that controlling shareholders, who because of their power obtain and trade upon private corporation information, should be liable to their

[21] 213 U.S. 419, 431-32 (1909).
[22] *Supra* note 19, at 1448.

fellow shareholders to the same extent as corporate officers or directors. The opportunity to test this question came in *Geller v. Transamerica Corporation.*[23] As dominant shareholder in a tobacco company, Transamerica received inside information that the cash value of the company's tobacco inventory was far greater than that stated in the published financial reports. Acting on this information, Transamerica caused the company to call in plaintiff's shares at a price higher than the market but much below the liquidating value of the stock. Then, holding the plaintiff's shares as well as those of other minority shareholders, Transamerica effected a sale of the tobacco to another enterprise and, consequently, the liquidation of the tobacco company. Following the so-called majority view, the court rejected the plaintiff's common-law suit for deceit.

For other injured persons, however, relief was available in the form of the SEC's rule 10b-5, which we have already discussed.[24] The facts alleged in *Geller,* which failed to state a cause of action for common-law fraud, constituted a violation of the Commission's rule, for which the plaintiffs were entitled to recovery. The defendant controlling shareholders had failed to disclose a "material fact" necessary to make the facts stated not misleading, in connection with the purchase of a security.

Today only a slight extension of this rule is necessary to bring institutional investors within its grasp. Tomorrow the facts may be such that there will be no question of the rule's application. For the present there is the problem of defining the institutional investor as an "insider," for the duty of disclosure apparently applies only to that class. Professor Loss would consider an insider "a person who picks up private information in the course of business negotiations with a corporation—perhaps negotiations to buy the corporation's assets or the management's stock."[25] And he would consider that person an insider "so long as that information remains private."

A very recent suit by the Securities and Exchange Commission against Texas Gulf Sulphur Company and certain of its officers, directors, and employees may very well provide a theoretical basis

---

[23] 53 F. Supp. 625 (D. Del. 1943), *aff'd per curiam,* 151 F.2d 534 (3d Cir. 1945).

[24] Speed v. Transamerica, 135 F. Supp. 176 (D. Del. 1955), *modified,* 235 F.2d 369 (3d Cir. 1956).

[25] *Supra* note 19, at 1451.

for establishing liability where insiders disclose confidential information to others, such as institutions, who act on such information by trading in the company's stock. The SEC's complaint alleges that certain insiders of Texas Gulf, who had knowledge of an extremely valuable ore strike by the company in Timmins, Ontario, bought shares of their company's stock in the open market at a time when information regarding the strike was not generally available, and that the insiders failed to disclose this information to the persons from whom they purchased such shares. The complaint also alleges that one employee and two directors disclosed this information to outsiders, including one very large bank, who purchased Texas Gulf shares without disclosing this valuable information to the persons from whom they purchased. Significantly, the SEC's complaint charges the insiders who "leaked" the information with violations of rule 10b-5, and seeks to hold them, rather than their "tippees," liable in damages to persons who sold their Texas Gulf stock in ignorance of the company's ore strike. If the SEC is successful in establishing the principle that insiders may be liable for breaching their fiduciary duties by wrongfully disclosing confidential corporate information, the institutions' access to such information may be significantly curtailed.

One could speculate, too, on the problem of sale of control raised earlier in the discussion of *Perlman v. Feldmann*. The future may find groups of institutions with clear working control in some of their portfolio corporations. The control may exist only if the holdings of several institutions are combined. Nevertheless, duties may be imposed on the passing of control. Certainly the law now would cover the sale of control when financial institutions act in concert to sell control—the "corporate asset"—at a high premium. The future may find the law operating on the institutions without there having to be concert of action.

Suppose thirty institutions held equal blocks of stock in a portfolio corporation, amounting to 30 per cent of that corporation's outstanding stock. Without conspiracy, without meeting as a body with the prospective purchaser, each institution, with knowledge of the sales of others, sold its 1-per-cent-block to the same buyer at a premium. From this fact pattern the courts may find that the institutions owed certain responsibilities to their fellow shareholders in the portfolio corporation. Each institution possessed in its holdings an essential element for working control. This the buyer realized from his payment of a premium. If the sale was to one bent on looting the corporation, should not each institution be held to account, at least to the extent of being required to investigate the background of the buyer? With their credit-checking facilities, this is a task that institutions easily could accomplish. Even if the sale has not been injurious to the corporation, the institutions may still be required to account for the premium paid for their shares. The reasoning for this conclusion is much the same as in *Perlman v. Feldmann* but finds its roots in the principle that with power goes responsibility.

From the common law and the development of federal securities legislation come the principles that may form the nucleus for the imposition of broader fiduciary standards of institutional conduct with respect to portfolio corporations. These principles are not new; they are tested concepts that have evolved slowly over the years. They are but a refinement of the mandate requiring fair dealing.

Only the facts described and placed in context are new. The growth and development of institutional power is a continuing, changing process. And it is to these facts that the law will be applied. The resulting conclusions as cases arise should frame a policy that will benefit the institutions themselves, for the development of legal standards for the responsible use of the great power that institutions are accumulating—indeed, already possess—can unleash a powerful force for broader shareholder democracy, more effective business management, and a stronger, healthier economy.

TABLE OF CASES

INDEX